FANTASY AND REALITY

FANTASY AND REALITY

Drawings from the Sunny Crawford von Bülow Collection

Cara Dufour Denison

With contributions by

Stephanie Wiles and Ruth S. Kraemer

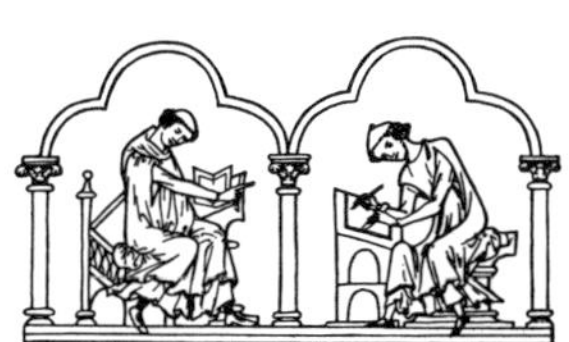

THE PIERPONT MORGAN LIBRARY · NEW YORK · 1995

The Pierpont Morgan Library, New York
14 September 1995–7 January 1996

Published in 1995 by
The Pierpont Morgan Library
29 East 36th Street
New York, New York 10016

Library of Congress Cataloging-in-Publication Data

Denison, Cara D.
Fantasy and reality : drawings from the Sunny Crawford von Bülow collection / Cara Denison ; with contributions by Stephanie Wiles and Ruth Kraemer.
p. cm.
Catalog of an exhibition held at the Pierpont Morgan Library.
Includes index.
ISBN 0-87598-114-3 (alk. paper)
1. Drawing—Exhibitions. 2. Von Bülow, Martha Crawford, 1931– —Art collections—Exhibitions. 3. Drawing—New York (N.Y.)—Exhibitions. 4. Pierpont Morgan Library—Exhibitions. I. Wiles, Stephanie. II. Kraemer, Ruth S. III. Pierpont Morgan Library. IV. Title.
NC25.N4D46 1995
741.94'09'0330747471—dc20 95-431
CIP

Photography of Morgan Library collection materials
by David A. Loggie

Distributed by University of Washington Press
P.O. Box 50096, Seattle, Washington 98415

Cover: Jean-Baptiste Oudry, *The Rond-Point in the Park at Arcueil* (No. 4).

Acknowledgments

The authors would like to thank their colleagues in the Department of Drawings and Prints, William M. Griswold, Evelyn J. Phimister, and Felice Stampfle, Curator Emerita, as well as the following: Evan Baker, Bruno de Bayser, Adrian Eeles, David Jones, Robert Manning, Marianne Roland Michel, John A. Pinto, Alan Salz, Alice Schreyer, Judith Schub, Arlette Sérullaz, and Lindsay Stainton. Other curators and staff members of the Library were generous with their time and expertise, including: Dr. Anna Lou Ashby, H. George Fletcher, Elizabeth O'Keefe, Kay Brooks, Paolina Taglienti, Inge Dupont, Katherine Reagan, and Kevin Pluta. This catalogue has been greatly facilitated by Kathleen Stuart, who served as research assistant and editorial liaison. We are also grateful to Jennifer Tonkavich, who worked as an intern. Special thanks are owed to Timothy Herstein, who prepared French mats for nearly all the drawings in the exhibition.

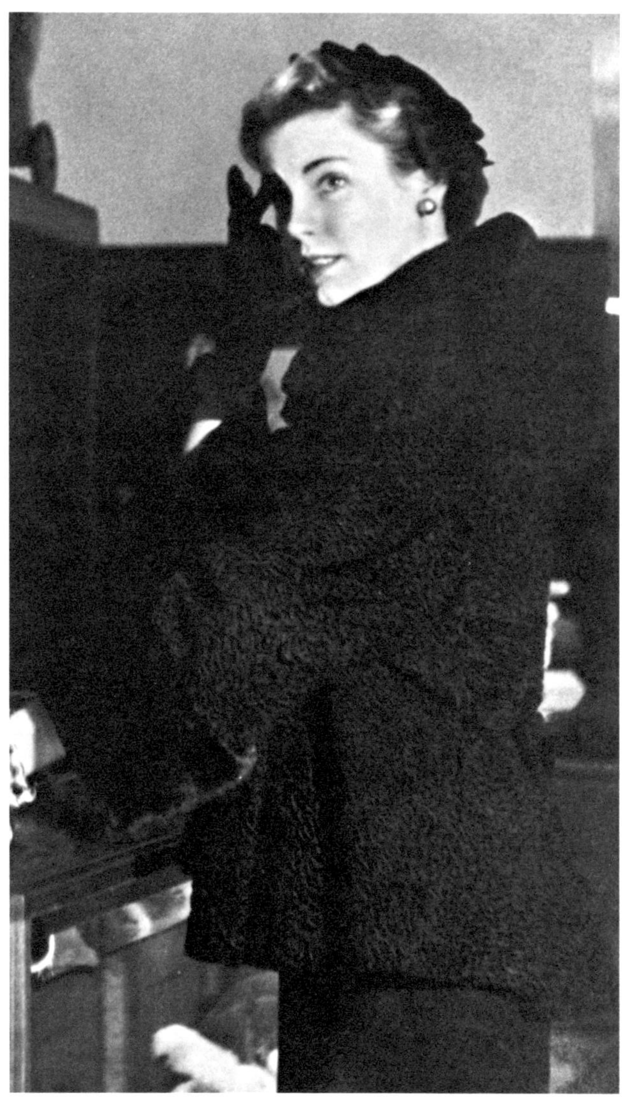

Sunny Crawford von Bülow

Foreword

In the 1970s Sunny Crawford von Bülow had already established herself as a person of notable taste. The von Bülows' house at Newport and their great apartment in New York were legendary for their furniture, books, and decorative arts.

For The Metropolitan Museum of Art, she purchased, among other things, *The Four Continents*, a magnificent set of Beauvais tapestries. At the same time, Mrs. von Bülow began a series of annual purchases of drawings and watercolors for The Pierpont Morgan Library. Her friendship with the then director, Charles Ryskamp, and the guidance she received from the late David Carritt in London were important factors in turning her in this direction.

Mrs. von Bülow took a strong personal interest in each drawing that was acquired with her funds. She wanted them to reflect her own areas of interest and to form someday a harmonious group while also filling significant gaps in the Library's holdings.

When tragedy struck, and she was no longer able to carry on with such interests or activities, it fell to her fiduciaries and her children to dispose of the charitable funds for which she had carefully provided continuity. Among her three children, it was Cosima von Bülow, her youngest child, who, remembering the pleasure her mother took in the Morgan Library project, decided to continue it in her name and has done so over these last fourteen years. It is to Cosima's dedication that this outstanding group of drawings is primarily due.

Knowing full well her mother's eye and preferences, Cosima also saw to it, as well as she could, that the Library's purchases on her mother's fund would conform to the style she had established rather than be made across the board for all kinds of drawings that might be of scholarly import but would disrupt the cohesive nature of the collection. Primarily comprised of eighteenth-century drawings, the collection neatly juxtaposes the taste for rococo fantasy with the austere realism of neoclassicism. The brilliance of Watteau's red-chalk *Temple of Diana* and the magical charm of Oudry's *Rond-Point in the Park at Arcueil* contrast markedly with the forthright immediacy of Ingres's pencil portrait of Charles Désiré Norry and the hyperrealism of Hüet's modern still life *Studies of Corn Husks and Wheat.* The Library curators have been equally mindful of this unity of taste in their recommendations. With one or two exceptions, this preference has been respected, and, happily, many of these drawings have indeed filled important gaps in the Library's earlier holdings. Fourteen of the Library's 125 most important French drawings, which were exhibited at the Louvre in 1993, were gifts from the Sunny Crawford von Bülow Fund 1978.

Recently, in a period of astronomical market prices, the Library has acquired an extraordinary number of drawings that it would not have been able to afford. The Janos Scholz bequest of Italian drawings, the promise of Mrs. Rudolf J. Heinemann's beautiful Tiepolos, the gifts of Mrs. Herbert N. Straus, the John S. Thacher bequest of Delacroix and Degas, the Thaw Collection, and the Sunny Crawford von Bülow Fund 1978 have more than compensated for the absence of a comparable acquisitions endowment.

This exhibition is an accounting of what has been accomplished in Sunny von Bülow's name so far. It is the fervent wish of the Library's staff, Trustees, Fellows, and Friends that this important purchasing fund—by far the Library's most significant—be continued and that, after the passage of time, another, even more comprehensive, von Bülow exhibition be mounted. In the meantime, it is with great pride and pleasure that we present to the public this important and beautiful collection. It cannot help but delight the eye and stimulate the mind.

Charles E. Pierce, Jr.
Director, The Pierpont Morgan Library

Catalogue of Drawings

1

JEAN ANTOINE WATTEAU

Valenciennes 1684–1721 Nogent-sur-Marne

River Landscape with a Fortified Town and Distant Mountains

Red chalk. 13 x 18 5/16 inches (330 x 465 mm). Watermark: coat of arms with serpent (close to Heawood 688).

PROVENANCE: Camille Groult; J. Groult; P. Bordeaux-Groult; Didier Aaron, New York; sale, Lille, 13 March 1994, lot 27, repr. (in color); Galerie Schmit, Paris.

BIBLIOGRAPHY: Parker and Mathey 1957, I, p. 52, no. 442, repr.; London 1980, under no. 15; Washington 1988–89, p. 180 n. 86.

EXHIBITION: New York 1984, no. 47, repr.

1995.1

This large drawing—the largest known by the artist—may be one of 100 copies Watteau made after Venetian drawings by Titian and Campagnola acquired in 1715 by Pierre Crozat, the great patron of the arts and collector. One of Crozat's friends was the French art historian and theorist Roger de Piles (1635–1709). In his history, De Piles expanded the concept of history painting to include many different types of subjects describing the Venetian landscape as a separate artistic category, recommending that the Venetian masters' drawings and prints be copied directly in order to grasp their expressive potential. To De Piles, the essential aspects of Venetian pastorals included "figures, animals, rivers or streams, trees rustled by the wind, and lightness of the brush." That Watteau copied them is well documented by Mariette in his *Abecedario* as well as reported by Caylus, who was also a member of the circle that gathered at Crozat's house. It was Caylus who observed that Watteau was so interested in the landscapes of Titian and Campagnola and impressed by their inventions that he assiduously copied their drawings and prints. Watteau's red chalk, however, gave a softer and more atmospheric character to the essentially dry pen rendering of Campagnola's landscapes.

The work that Watteau copied in this drawing—most likely a Campagnola—is not known. Although he is said to have copied a hundred drawings from Crozat's collection, not all of these are known (Parker and Mathey 1957, I, pp. 51–58, nos. 368–443). Moreover, Watteau is known to have copied works in the Cabinet du Roi as well, but these sources have yet to be conclusively identified. A volume containing a sampling of works then in the French royal collection (*Recueil de 283 estampes gravées a l'eau forte par les plus habiles peintres . . .* , Paris, 1754) includes designs with numerous elements similar to this drawing, but none is particularly close. While not exact, Watteau's *River Landscape* does conform in many respects to the Campagnola print *Landscape with Wandering Family*, inscribed "Cab. du Roy" (fig. 1; B. 4; see *Tizian und sein Kreis*, catalogue by Peter Dreyer, Berlin, [n.d.], no. 33, repr.). The form of the distant mountains, the curve of the waterway, the high vantage point with the crouching figures, and even a number of the buildings and bridges in the print are paralleled in this drawing.

Watteau evidently so liked the mountainous background here that he adapted it freely in his *Le Pélerinage à l'isle de Cithère*, in which the mountains are quite similar and have been repositioned more centrally so as to be directly behind the river or lake that also appears in the painting. The shoreline of this body of water, along with the high viewpoint of the figures in the foreground, is similar in both compositions. Watteau also used the mountain motif for *Fête d'Amour*, a painting in Dresden. In this work, the position, if not quite the pose, of the seated warrior in the drawing is repeated above the landscape. CDD

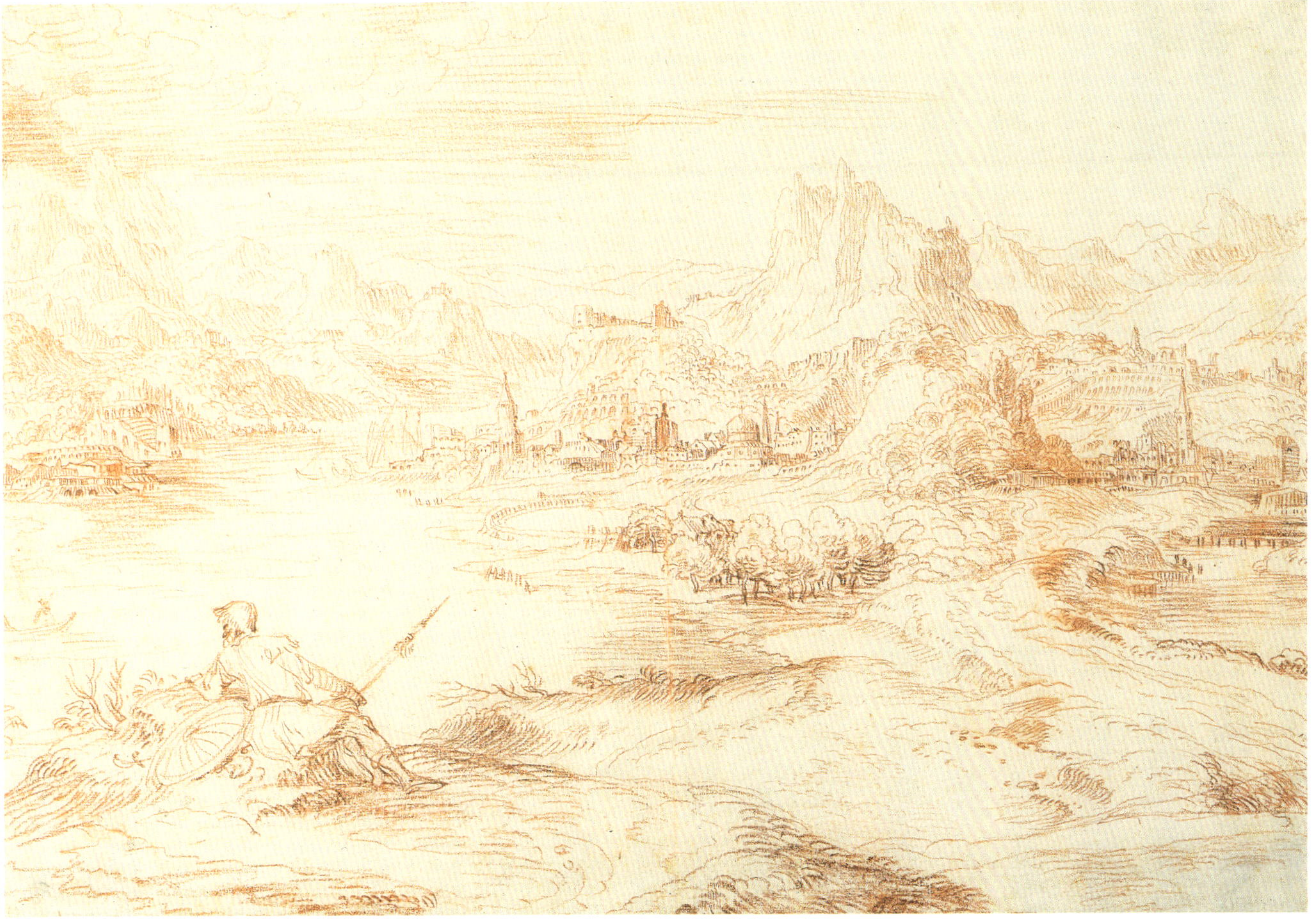

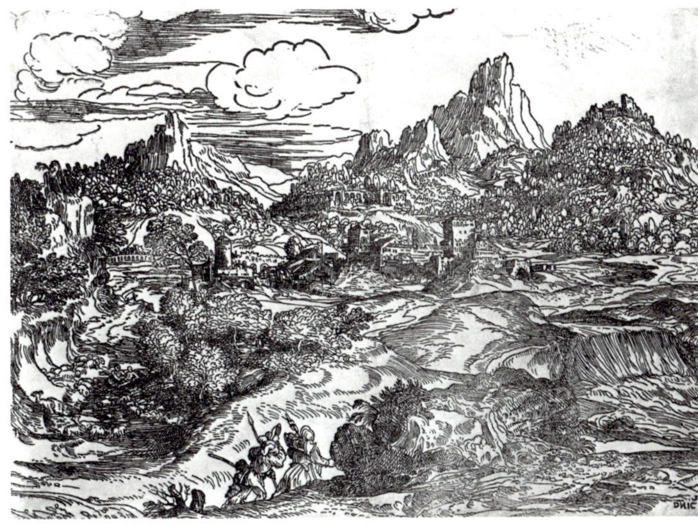

Fig. 1 Domenico Campagnola, *Landscape with Wandering Family*, The Metropolitan Museum of Art, New York, 67.770.

2

JEAN ANTOINE WATTEAU

Valenciennes 1684–1721 Nogent-sur-Marne

The Temple of Diana

Red chalk. 10 1/2 x 14 1/4 inches (267 x 362 mm). Watermark: fragment of chaplet (cf. Heawood 222).

PROVENANCE: possibly Gabriel Huquier (as plausibly suggested by Martin Eidelberg); Edmond and Jules de Goncourt (Lugt 1089); their sale, Paris, 15–17 February 1897, lot 350 (to Camille Groult for 250 frs.); Camille Groult; J. Groult.

BIBLIOGRAPHY: Goncourt 1875, p. 216, no. 279; Portalis and Béraldi 1880–82, p. 447 (mentions the prints); Fourcaud 1908–9, p. 131 n. 2; Deshairs 1913, p. 292; Réau 1928, p. 55, nos. 58, 59; Dacier and Vuaflart 1921–29, III, p. 103, under no. 225, repr.; Parker and Mathey 1957, I, p. 29, no. 191, repr.; Bruand and Hébert 1970, pp. 573f., nos. 1733–34; PML/*FR* XIX, 1981, p. 221; Eidelberg 1984, pp. 158, 160, 164 n. 9, fig. 3; Posner 1984, p. 61, colorpl. II; Michel 1984, p. 128, fig. LII (colorpl.); Michel 1987, pp. 137, 168, fig. 145; Grasselli 1993, p. 126 n. 12.

EXHIBITIONS: New York PML 1981, no. 98, repr.; New York 1984, no. 39, repr.; Washington and elsewhere 1984–85, p. 55, no. 71, repr.; Paris and New York 1993–94, no. 37, repr.

1980.9

While working with the ornamentalist Claude Audran, Watteau produced a number of designs for decorative arabesques. Under Audran's influence, Watteau became a practitioner of the newly emerging rococo style. He both painted and drew a number of decorative arabesques. Some have survived, and some are known only from the prints made after them in the *Recueil Jullienne,* which the noted collector Jean de Jullienne published between 1735 and 1738. As Marianne Roland Michel has remarked, Jullienne was motivated not only by the wish to memorialize his friend Watteau but also by the prospect of financial gain (see Michel 1984, p. 260). He directed his printmakers to multiply the number of drawn or painted arabesques to around fifty. A number of Watteau's drawings of arabesques were actually produced subsequent to the Audran years, which their relation to paintings of later date makes apparent (Washington and elsewhere 1984–85, p. 55). The present drawing must have been executed around 1716 because of its stylistic similarity to *The Bower,* which is connected to a painting of 1716 and is now in the National Gallery of Art, Washington, D.C. (fig. 1).

The artist's inventiveness is displayed in the proliferation of decorative motives and ideas in this drawing. They came to him so rapidly that he summarily sketched in alternates. At the center, Diana and attendant nymphs are seen on a pedestal under a leafy arch topped by a stag's head that divides the design into halves. At one side, the arch becomes a rococo arbor supported by herms; at the other it is transformed into a stone structure culminating in a fantastic shell-like decoration. This side is supported by a column with a putto perched on a fountain; a vase motif emerges from a bracket. To the right, elegant couples, including a nymph and satyr, are lightly sketched. On the left, two whippets pose atop a line of tracery under which suspends a net looped at the center through a circular hunting horn. Birds fly above.

Huquier derived two prints from Watteau's design, *The Temple of Diana* (Dacier and Vuaflart 1921–29, III, no. 225) and *The Temple of Neptune* (ibid, I, no. 224). In the latter, Huquier supplied the figure of Neptune, absent in Watteau's drawing, and completed the rusticated arch motif in conjunction with the bracketed vase, nymphs, and satyrs. In *The Temple of Diana,* he developed Watteau's other solution for the arbor, or trellis, using the herms and nymphs along with the hunting horn and nets while balancing Watteau's whippets with a running stag of his own invention. Martin Eidelberg (1984) notes that Huquier's prints, inscribed *A. Watteau Invenit,* are entirely different in character from the Watteau original—pastiches rather than faithful extensions of Watteau's designs. In aspiring to develop the draughtsman's alternate suggestions, the resulting prints are in fact quite different from Watteau's artistic intention. CDD

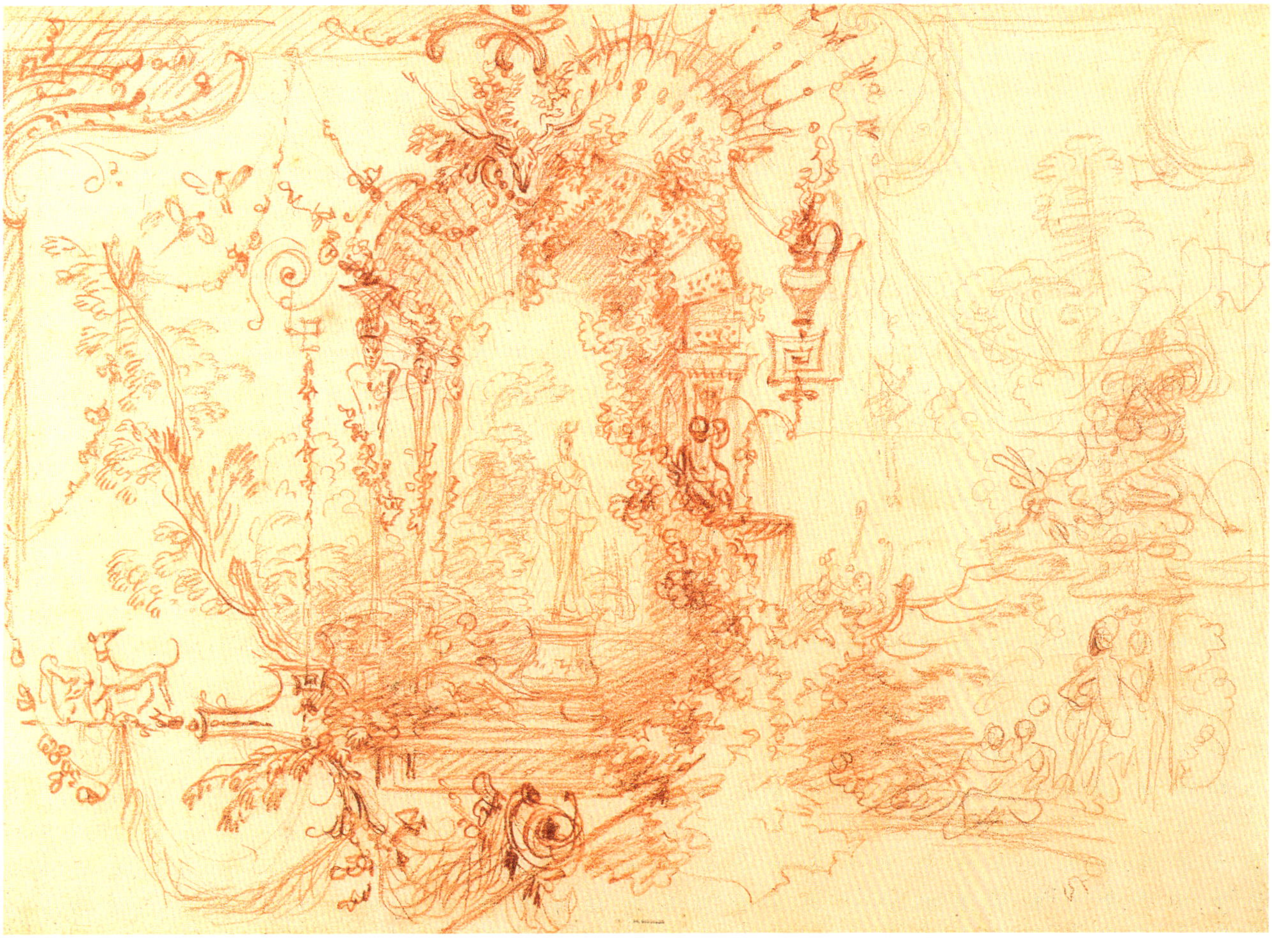

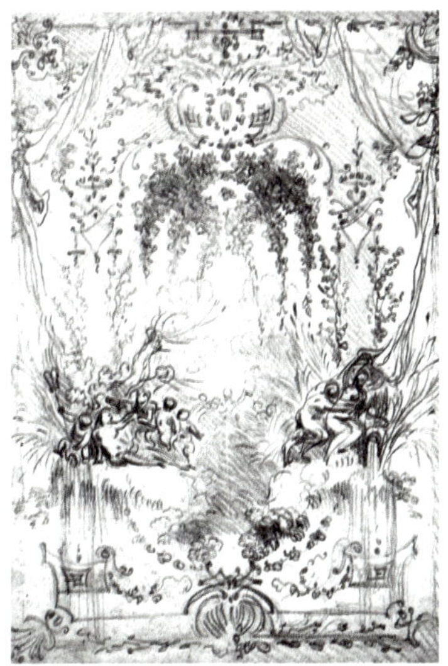

Fig. 1 Jean Antoine Watteau, *The Bower*, National Gallery of Art, Washington, D.C., 1982.72.1.

3

JEAN ANTOINE WATTEAU

Valenciennes 1684–1721 Nogent-sur-Marne

Study of a Shell (*Cassis inflata*)

Red and black chalk. 8 7/8 x 8 1/4 inches (226 x 208 mm). Watermark: none. Inscribed on verso in red chalk, *Watteau*.

PROVENANCE: Camille Groult, Paris; J. Groult, Paris; P. Bordeaux-Groult, Paris; David Carritt Limited, London.

BIBLIOGRAPHY: Parker and Mathey 1957, II, p. 369, no. 905, repr.; Paris and Amsterdam 1964, p. 37; Cambridge and elsewhere 1980, under no. 35; PML/*FR* XIX, 1981, p. 221; Sérullaz 1981, p. 32 and n. 16; Washington and elsewhere 1984–85, p. 55; Paris 1987, under no. 111.

EXHIBITION: London 1978, no. 19, repr.

1978.29

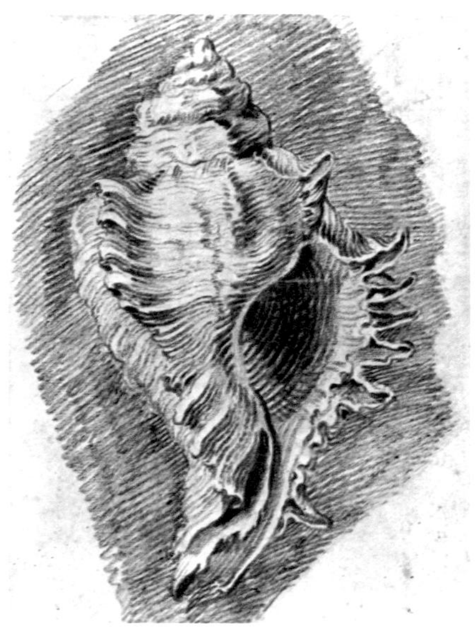

Fig. 1 Jean Antoine Watteau, *Murex anguliferus*, Collection Frits Lugt, Institut Néerlandais, Paris, Inv. 7634.

This drawing is one of only seven known studies of tropical shells by the artist (Parker and Mathey 1957, II, nos. 901–7). The studies are generally believed to have been drawn in 1720, when, after a severe winter in London, Watteau, whose consumption had worsened, returned to Paris to convalesce on the Pont Notre-Dame at the home of his friend, the wealthy picture dealer Gersaint, for whom he painted the famous *Enseigne*. Gersaint's curiosity collection included seashells; in fact, he seems to have been one of the first enthusiasts and dealers to spread the taste for exotic examples. Each year he made a trip to the Netherlands to replenish his stock of shells for his shop. The other six studies include three in Besançon (*Murex anguliferus*, *Strombus occipitrinus*, and both *Cypraea tigris* and *Cypraea mappa* on the same sheet; fig. 2) and one each at the Louvre (a double study of *Pterocerra rugosa*), the Institut Néerlandais, Paris (another study of *Murex anguliferus;* fig. 1), and the Berlin printroom (*Strombus occipitrinus*).

It has been suggested that these drawings are not by Watteau and might be attributed instead to his successor François Boucher, whose works document his life-long fascination with shells and who was commissioned in 1736 to design the frontispiece of the *Catalogue raisonné de coquilles et autres curiosités naturelles* (Maurice Roux, *Bibliothèque Nationale, Département des Estampes, Inventaire du fonds français, graveurs du XVIIIème siècle*, VIII, Paris, 1955, p. 59; Cambridge and elsewhere 1980, no. 35). While the suggestion is attractive, given certain of Boucher's stylistic affinities, it has yet to be proven or espoused by current Watteau specialists. Pierre Rosenberg and Margaret Morgan Grasselli neither accept the traditional attribution of this group of drawings to Watteau nor propose another (Washington and elsewhere 1984–85, p. 55). They feel that the ornamental handling of the contours and modeling suggest that the group is the work of a designer of decorative pieces, perhaps a sculptor. They also note that there is no parallel in Watteau's work for the execution of the hatched backgrounds or the distinct separation of the red and black chalks. Recently, however, the authors of a Louvre catalogue (Paris 1987), regretting that the group had not been exhibited in the 1984 Watteau exhibition (Washington and elsewhere 1984–85), rejected these conclusions and upheld the attribution to Watteau. CDD

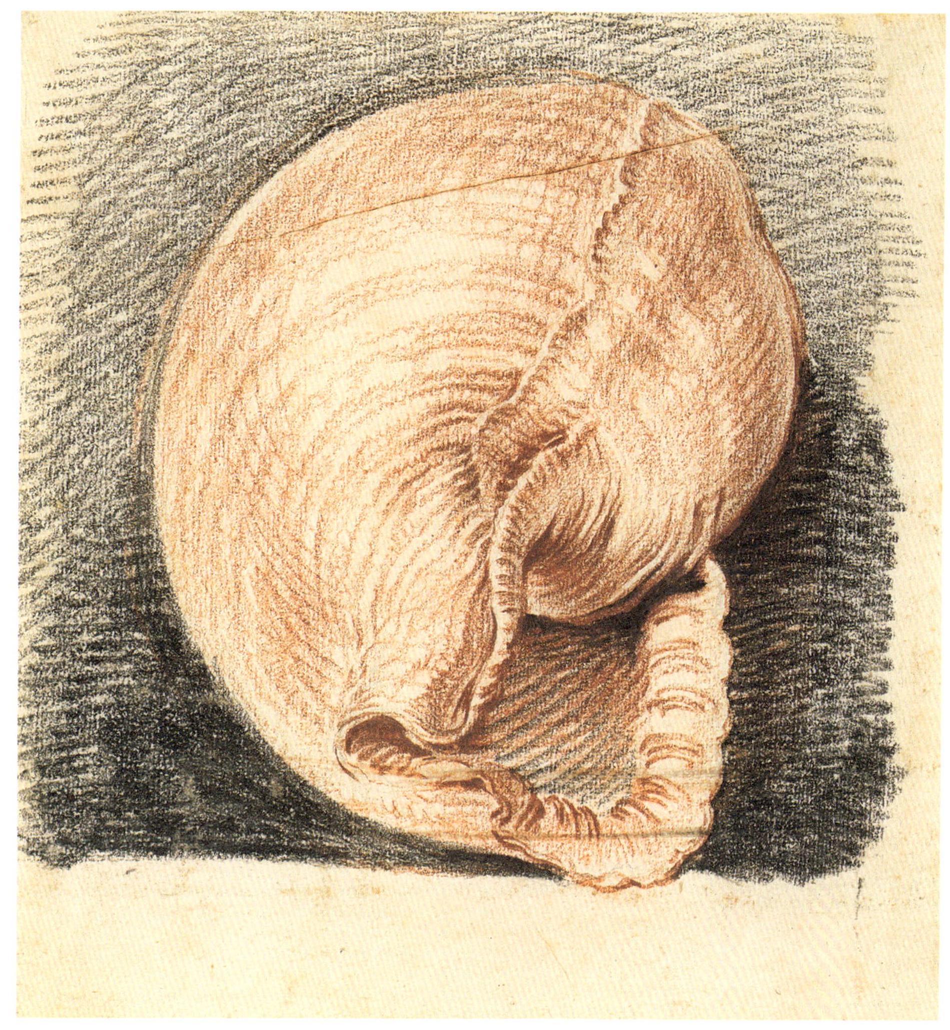

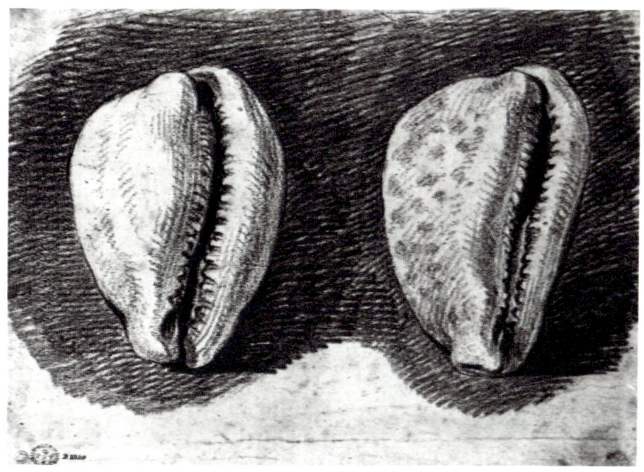

Fig. 2 Jean Antoine Watteau, *Cypraea tigris* and *Cypraea mappa*, Musée des Beaux-Arts et d'Archéologie, Besançon, D. 2320.

4

JEAN-BAPTISTE OUDRY

Paris 1686–1755 Beauvais

The Rond-Point in the Park at Arcueil

Black chalks (two shades), heightened with white, in places gone over with a wet brush or stumped, on blue paper; traces of a ruled border in black ink. 11 13/16 x 20 1/4 inches (302 x 523 mm). Watermark: fragment with letters M GIS.

PROVENANCE: E. Desperet (Lugt 721); his sale, Paris, Hôtel Drouot, 7–13 June 1865, part of no. 449 (62 frs., to Noizy); Jean Masson (Lugt 1494a); his sale, Paris, Galerie Georges Petit, 7–8 May 1923, lot 177, repr. (1,050 frs.), to Meyer Bleneau; Katrin Bellinger, Munich.

BIBLIOGRAPHY: Desguine 1950, p. 9, pl. 5; Opperman 1977, II, p. 862, no. D1087.

EXHIBITIONS: London 1990b, no. 33, repr., and on cover (both in color); New York 1990, no. 25, repr. (in color); Paris and New York 1993–94, no. 40, repr. (in color).

1990.24

This is one of a group of at least fifty extant views executed by Oudry between 1744 and 1747, when he lived near the small château and gardens of the prince de Guise at Arcueil, near Paris. Most of these drawings are in European public collections: four are in the Louvre, one each is in the Musée Carnavalet and the Ecole des Beaux-Arts, two are in the Musée de l'Ile-de-France at Sceaux, and one is in the Albertina (see fig. 1). One other view is in New York at The Metropolitan Museum of Art.

Known primarily as a painter of still lifes, Oudry received his early training from Largillière and was made director of the tapestry works at Beauvais in 1744. It was there that his interest in landscape developed, and he subsequently produced these views, which are generally counted among his major achievements as a draughtsman. Contemporary sources tell us that the gardens of Arcueil, already neglected at this time, offered new inspiration for many artists, including Boucher, Natoire, Pierre, Portail, and Wille. The picturesque ruin and romantic charm of Arcueil seem to have especially appealed to Oudry, who is believed to have produced some one hundred views of the park.

This drawing was one of four views of parks by Oudry that were sold in the 1923 Masson sale. The complexity of the media makes it likely that Oudry made only a simple black chalk sketch on the spot and later reworked it in a mixture of point of brush and another type of black chalk, which he partially stumped. The monumental garden staircase can be seen in the background, leading up to the parterre with a balustrade directly in front of the château, which is not visible. The park is empty, giving the view a somewhat unearthly, almost surreal, air. A number of Oudry's Arcueil drawings were later reworked by Boilly, who added figural groups to the compositions. CDD

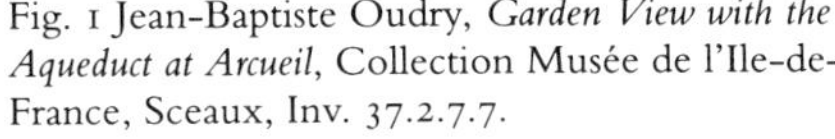

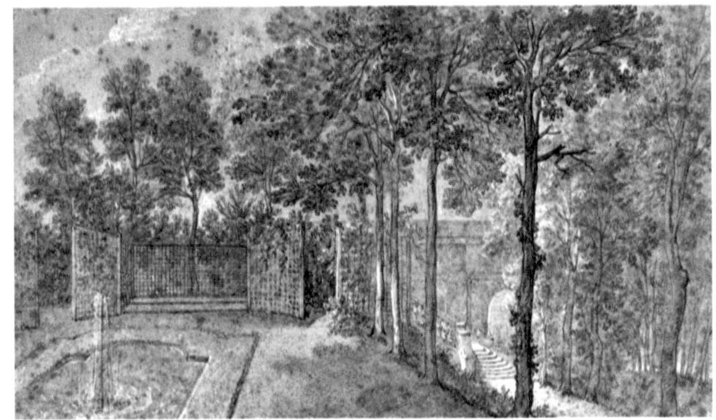

Fig. 1 Jean-Baptiste Oudry, *Garden View with the Aqueduct at Arcueil*, Collection Musée de l'Ile-de-France, Sceaux, Inv. 37.2.7.7.

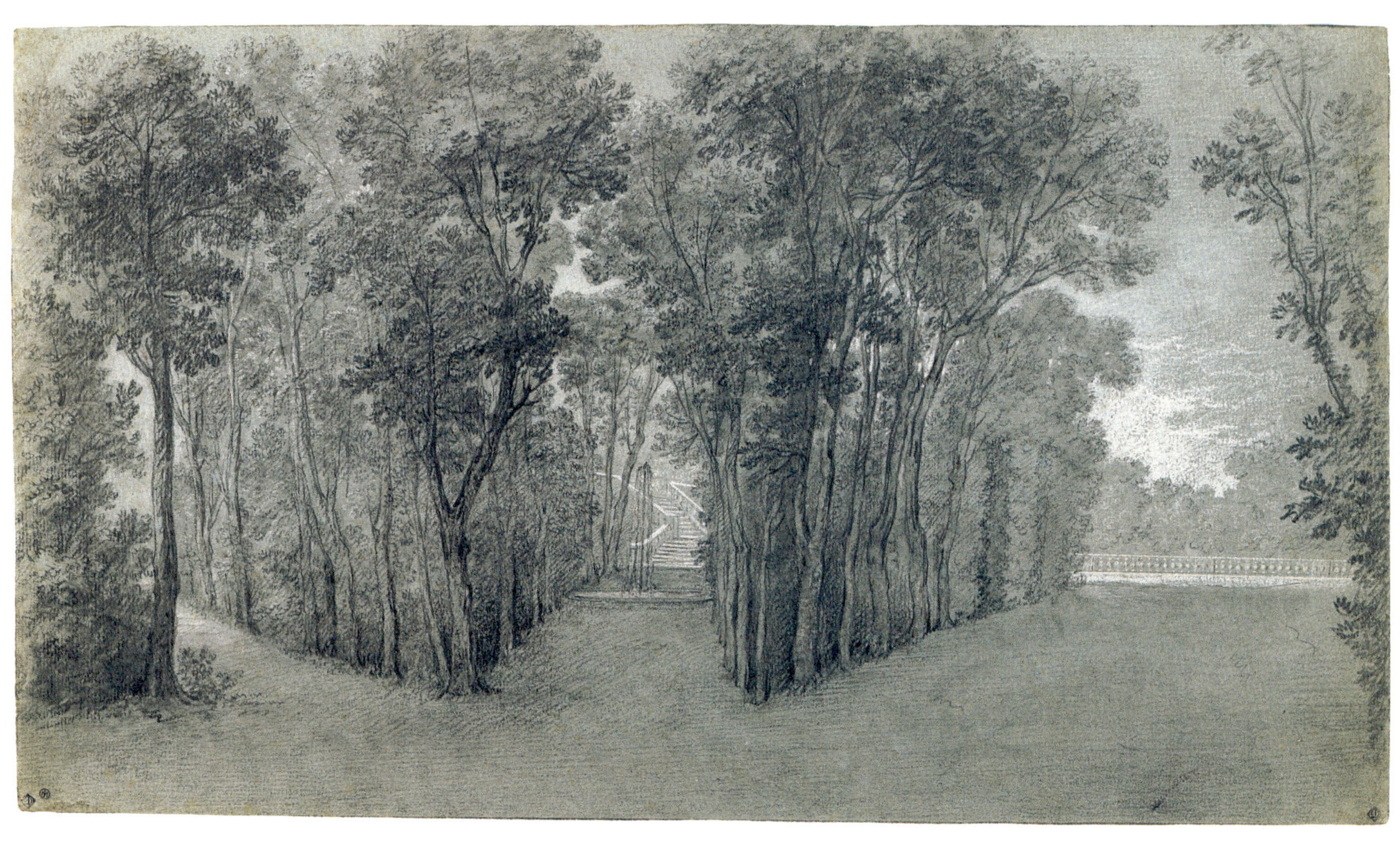

5

FRANÇOIS BOUCHER

Paris 1703–1770 Paris

Arion and the Dolphin

Pen and brown ink, brown wash, heightened with white, over black chalk, including some pentimenti, notably in Arion's head and in the prow of the ship, on blue paper. 7 15/16 x 11 5/8 inches (200 x 295 mm). Watermark: none visible through lining.

PROVENANCE: M. de Sireul *[sic]*, Paris; his sale, Paris, 3 December 1781, lot 88 (45 livres, 1 sol); M. Boulle; sale, London, Christie's, 10 December 1991, lot 204; Artemis Fine Arts, London.

BIBLIOGRAPHY: Michel 1889, no. 449; Ananoff 1966, no. 1006; Ananoff and Wildenstein 1976, II, under no. 328, fig. 953; Jean-Richard 1978, under no. 1443; New York and elsewhere 1986–87, under nos. 55, 56, p. 241 n. 1; Artemis 1993, p. 26, no. 10, repr. (in color).

EXHIBITION: Paris and New York 1993–94, no. 53, repr.

1991.45

In 1747 Louis XV commissioned Boucher to produce four paintings representing the elements for the Château de la Muette, near the Bois de Boulogne. This drawing is preparatory for the painting *Arion and the Dolphin*, dated 1748 and now in the Princeton University museum (fig. 1). Although the subject seems an unusual choice to represent the element of water, it was used in the Pierre-Charles Roy ballet *Les Eléments*, in which Louis XV himself performed in 1721. The artist completed only two paintings, *Arion and the Dolphin* and, to represent earth, *Vertumnus and Pomona*, now in the Columbus Museum of Art, Ohio (repr. New York and elsewhere 1986–87, no. 56), for which he was paid 1,400 livres on 28 September 1749. The series, originally designed for overdoors at La Muette, apparently never was installed since it is not mentioned in any of the contemporary descriptions of the château (see New York and elsewhere 1986–87, nos. 55, 56). The two paintings are mentioned again in the 1786 catalogue of the sale of M. Bergeret, who acquired them in 1764: "Deux charmantes compositions de cet artiste. L'une Vertumne et Pomone dans un riche fond de paysage et l'autre Arion porté sur un Dauphin jouant du luth, entouré de Tritons et Nayades: on voit plus loin le vaisseau qu'il vient d'abandonner."

The story of Arion and the dolphin comes from Herodotus: Arion, a Greek poet and musician, cast into the sea by pirates, was saved by a dolphin who heard the sound of his lyre. Both paintings were translated into engravings by Augustin de Saint-Aubin and Jean-Jacques Pasquier (repr. Jean-Richard 1978, no. 1443) in 1765 and 1766. In the 1781 de Sireul *[sic]* sale, this drawing was described as "Un superbe dessin. . . . Il représente Arion sur les flots, échappé au naufrage." While the high finish of the drawing indicates its probable use as a model for the painting, the charming nereid seen from the back in the foreground was eliminated in the painting. Her type and pose, however, are frequently found within Boucher's figural canon. This can be seen in several later works, including *Setting of the Sun*, dating to 1752 (Paris and elsewhere 1991–92, p. 485, fig. 3), particularly in the disposition of the figure and the inclination of her head, and in another study for the nudes in the foreground of Boucher's *Pan and Syrinx* of 1759 (repr. Ananoff and Wildenstein 1976, II, p. 192, no. 519/4, fig. 519/4). CDD

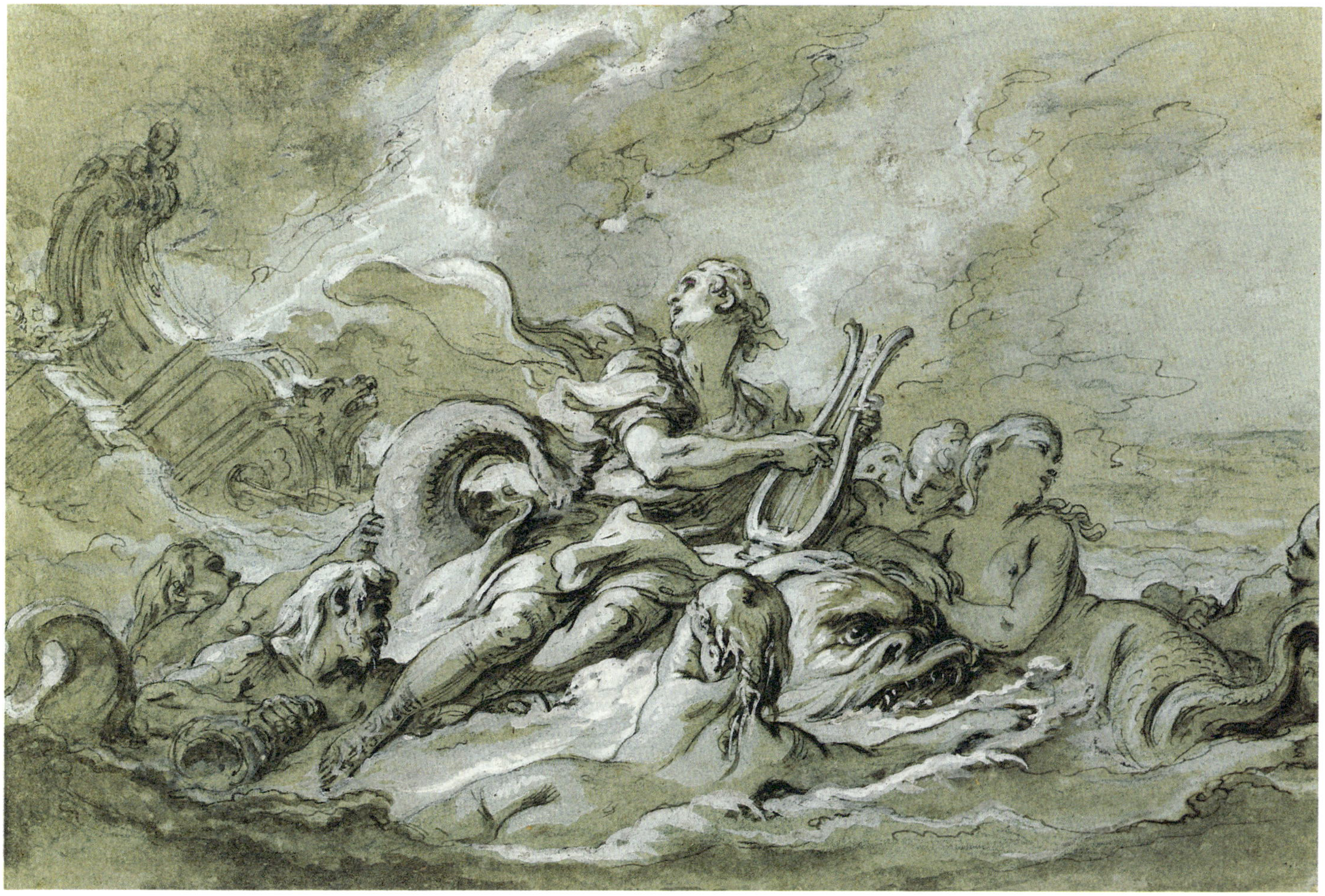

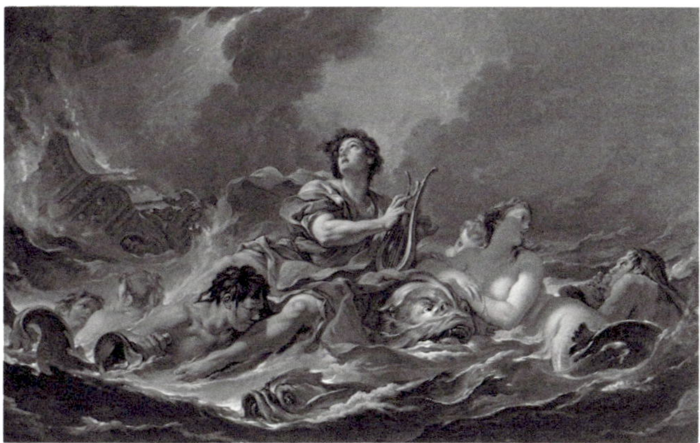

Fig. 1 François Boucher, *Arion and the Dolphin*, The Art Museum, Princeton University, Princeton, New Jersey, y1980-2.

6

FRANÇOIS BOUCHER

Paris 1703–1770 Paris

Young Woman in Classical Dress

Black chalk, heightened with white, on gray-blue paper, faded to light brown. 13 11/16 x 8 11/16 inches (348 x 222 mm). Watermark: none visible through lining.

PROVENANCE: Camille Groult; J. Groult; sale, Paris, Georges Petit, 21–22 June 1920, lot 130; Thos. Agnew & Sons, Ltd., London; C. R. Rudolf (Lugt S. 2811b); his sale, London, Sotheby's, 21 May 1963, lot 50, repr.; N. L. H. Roesler, New York; Mrs. Charles E. Slatkin, New York.

BIBLIOGRAPHY: Ananoff 1966, no. 755; PML/*FR* XX, 1984, pp. 239–40, fig. 25.

EXHIBITIONS: London 1953, no. 428; London 1962, no. 166, pl. 26; New York 1964, no. 10, repr.; Washington and Chicago 1973–74, no. 81, repr.; New York PML 1984, no. 50, repr.; Paris and New York 1993–94, no. 55, repr.

1983.1

This young woman's unusual costume, with its flowing robe, fringed stole, and turbanlike headdress, is very similar to those of both the Parthian princess and the queen of Syria in Boucher's study for the frontispiece to Corneille's tragedy *Rodogune,* which Madame de Pompadour had printed privately in 1759. The artist's drawing for this frontispiece has long been in the Morgan Library (fig. 1), and it is possible that this drawing is related to the same project. According to Regina Slatkin (Washington and Chicago 1973–74, nos. 80–81), at least two other drawings connected with Boucher's work on the Corneille publication are known. One, a black chalk sketch, was in the Jourdeuil collection (Lugt 527) and was sold at Christie's in the late 1960s (26 November 1968, lot 131). The other, in red chalk, heightened with Chinese white, was last seen in the Mühlbacher sale (1899, no. 90) and was at that time listed as *Rodogune. Scène à six personnages de la tragédie de Corneille. Illustration unique d'une édition publiée par Mme de Pompadour, en 1760.*

CDD

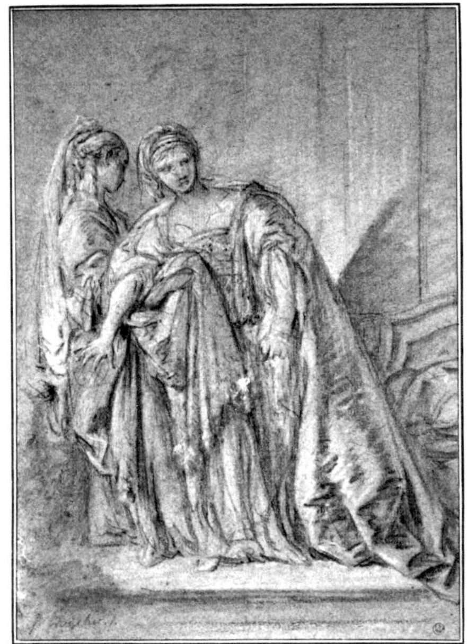

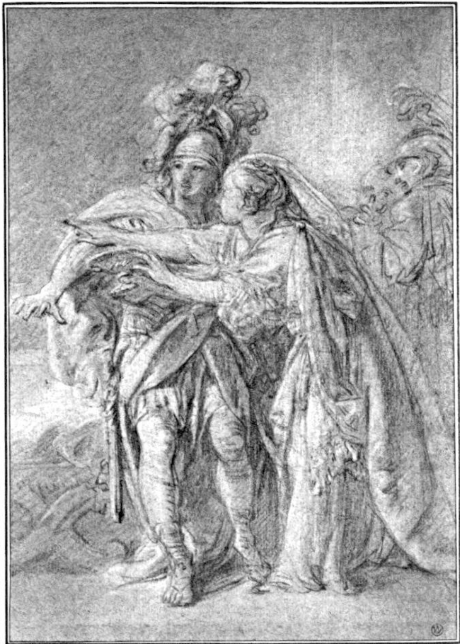

Fig. 1 François Boucher, *Rodogune,* The Pierpont Morgan Library, III,104a.

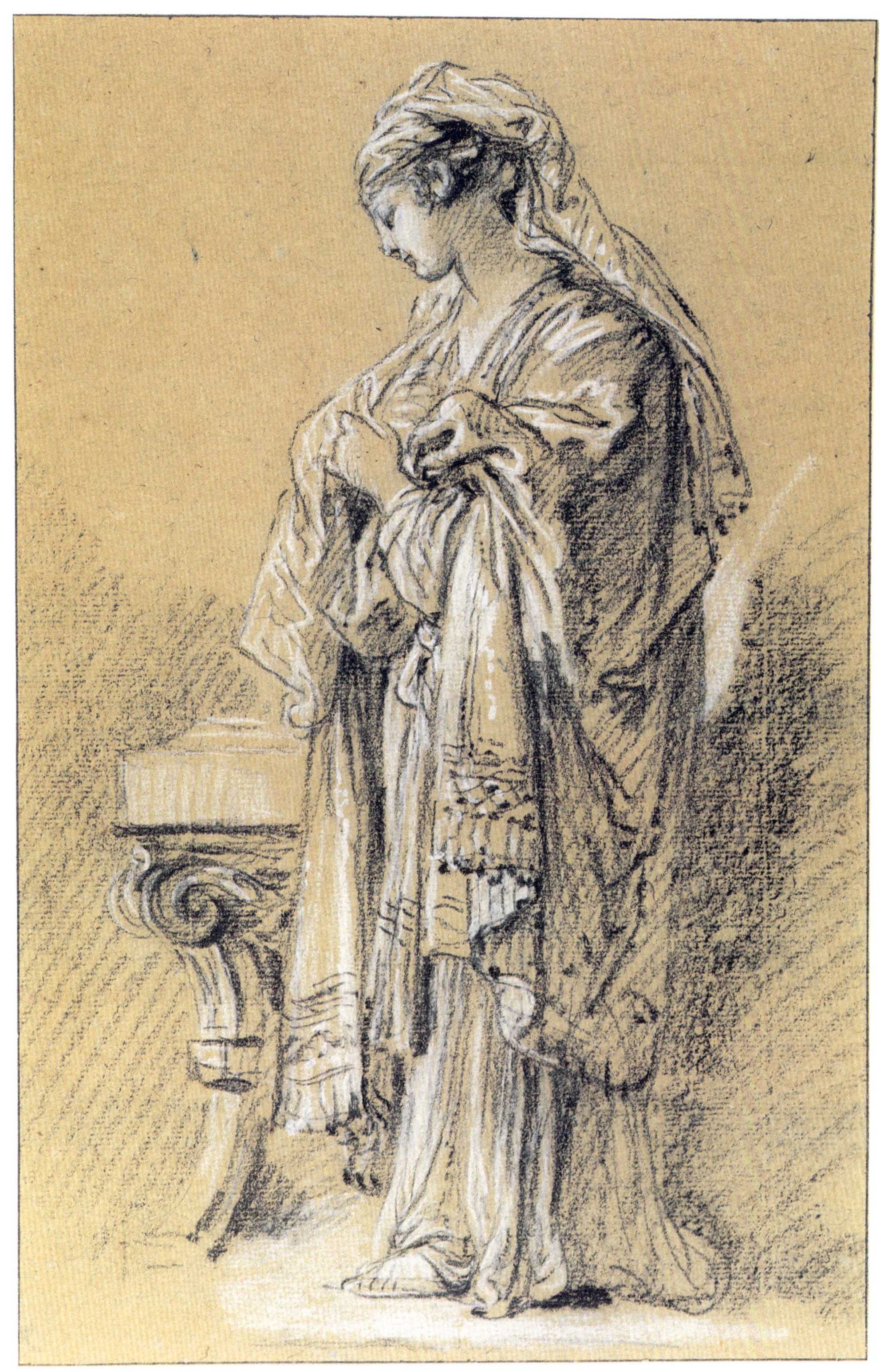

21

7

MAURICE QUENTIN DE LA TOUR

Saint-Quentin 1704–1788 Saint-Quentin

Portrait of Mlle Dangeville (Marie-Anne Botot, 1714–1796)

Colored chalks, stumped, on light blue paper. 11 1/4 x 9 1/8 inches (287 x 232 mm). Watermark: none visible through lining.

PROVENANCE: J. Auguste Carrier, Paris; his sale, Paris, Féral, 5 May 1875, lot 9; Mme Becq de Fouquières, Paris; David David-Weill, Neuilly; Mrs. Byron Foy, New York; private collection, New York; E. V. Thaw & Co., Inc., New York.

BIBLIOGRAPHY: Tourneux 1908, p. 9; Dacier 1913, [n.p.], repr.; Henriot 1925, p. 11, pl. XXI; Henriot 1927, pp. 29–30, repr.; Besnard and Wildenstein 1928, no. 92, pl. LXXII, fig. 127; Fleury and Brière 1954, p. 50, no. 13; PML/*FR* XX, 1984, p. 270.

EXHIBITIONS: Paris 1908, no. 30, repr. opp. p. 22; Paris 1927, no. 61; New York 1938, no. 7; New York PML 1984, no. 53; Paris and New York 1993–94, no. 56, repr.

1981.12

From 1730 until her retirement in 1763, Mlle Dangeville was a highly celebrated actress of the Comédie Française. As part of a theatrical family, she began her professional training at an early age. Although best known as a comédienne, it seems she played tragic roles with nearly equal facility since Voltaire cast her as Tullia in his *Brutus* of 1730. La Tour made three portraits of the actress in pastel. Two are in the Musée de Saint-Quentin; the other is in the Louvre (R.F. 4099). In this preparatory sketch for a full portrait, La Tour has already taken the full measure of the actress's personality. Her direct gaze seems to study the artist at work, a somewhat wicked smile enlivening her face. By all accounts, her face had considerable charm, and, although she was high-spirited and lively by nature, she was also tolerant and gracious. This portrait sketch was included in a major exhibition of pastels at the turn of this century, where it was described as "quelques coups de crayon de couleurs heurtées, de larges lumières à la craie, des balafres de sanguine et de noir, rien que cela, et c'est une tête. Vous regardez toujours: cette tête vient à vous, elle sort du cadre, elle s'enlève du papier et il vous semble n'avoir jamais vu dans aucun dessin de n'importe quelle école une pareille représentation d'une figure, quelque chose de crayonné qui fut autant quelqu'un de vivant."

In the 1920s Emile Dacier and Gabriel Henriot debated the identification of the sitter. M. Dacier doubted that the subject of this pastel could be the same lady depicted in the pastels at Saint-Quentin and in the Louvre. M. Henriot, however, maintained that there could be no doubt, especially if one compared this sketch with the busts of Dangeville in the Comédie Française executed by Jean-Baptiste Lemoyne and (unknown to M. Dacier) that by Defernex in the David-Weill collection, which is signed, inscribed, and dated *Melle Dangeville, par J.-Bte Defemeix, 1752*.

CDD

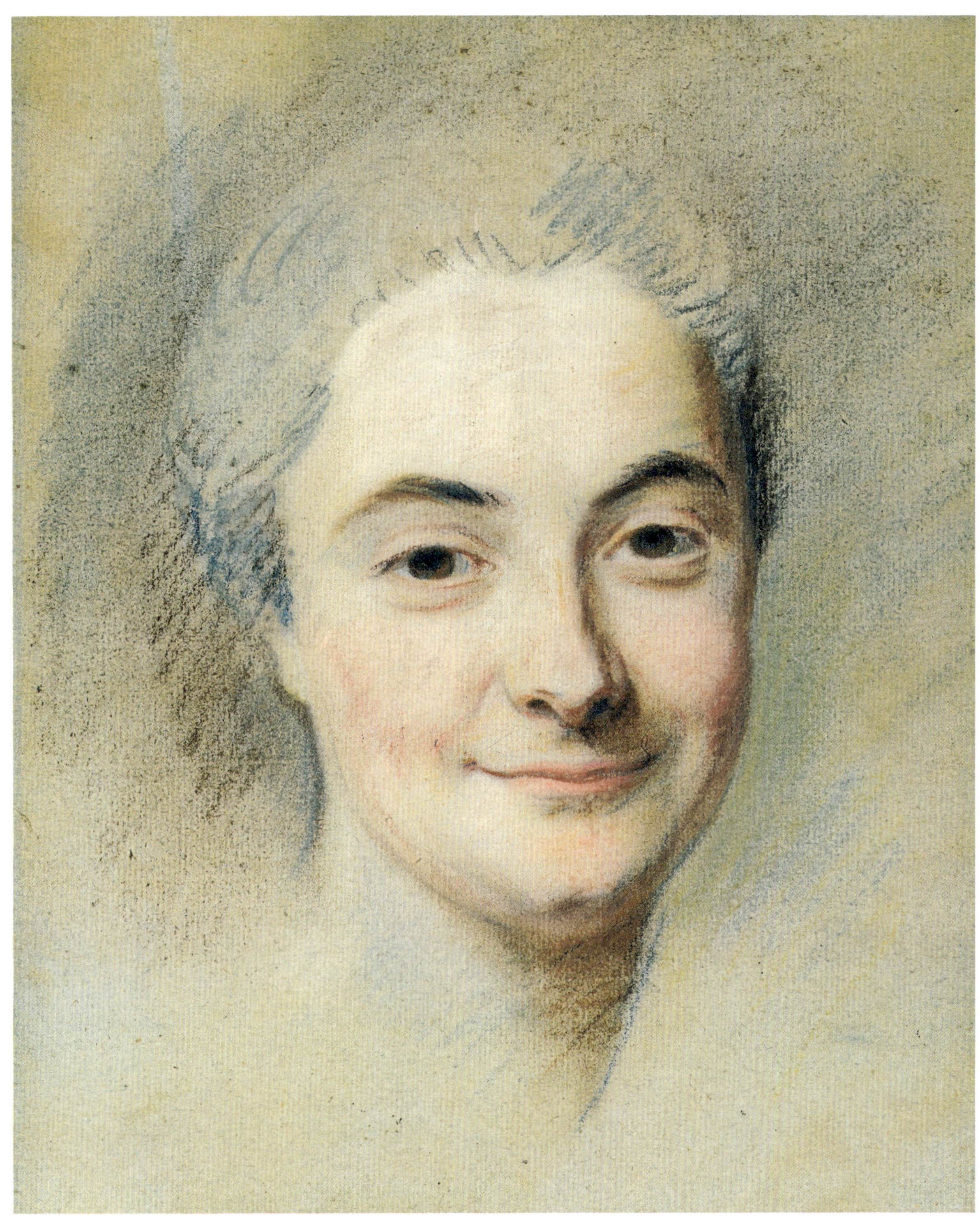

8

CARLE VAN LOO

Nice 1705–1765 Paris

Portrait of a Seated Woman, 1743

Black chalk, heightened with white, on blue paper. 18 5/16 x 12 13/16 inches (464 x 326 mm). Watermark: fleur-de-lis (cf. Heawood 1517). Signed and dated at lower left, in pen and brown ink, *Carle Vanloo 1743*.

PROVENANCE: Jean Masson (Lugt S. 1494a); his sale, Paris, Galerie Georges Petit, 7–8 May 1923, lot 232, repr. (800 frs.); M. Mohrange; sale, Casablanca, 25 March 1966, lot 32 (no catalogue); André Meyer, New York; his sale, New York, Sotheby Parke Bernet, 22 October 1980, lot 6, repr.; Richard J. Collins, Inc., New York; E. V. Thaw & Co., Inc., New York.

BIBLIOGRAPHY: Goncourt 1881, pp. 166–68; Toronto and elsewhere 1972–73, pp. 216–17, under no. 141; PML/*FR* XX, 1984, pp. 272–73.

EXHIBITIONS: Nice and elsewhere 1977, no. 409, repr.; New York PML 1984, no. 55; Paris and New York 1993–94, no. 58, repr.

1982.4

This portrait is one of a series of drawings by van Loo signed and dated 1743. Since the subjects of the six that we know—three men and three women—all sat for the artist in the same room, perhaps van Loo's atelier, it seems most probable that the artist was commissioned to make them.

It has not been possible to identify this lady or any of the other five subjects in the series, although Charles Dandré-Barton's early biography of van Loo (1765) refers to "Plusieurs portraits de la Famille & des amis de C. Vanloo, entre autres ceux des Dames Vanloo, & c. & des Messieurs Somis, Trémolières, Boucher, Dandré-Barton, & c." The portrait of a seated man was acquired by the Library earlier (fig. 1). The location of two of the remaining four is unknown. A portrait of a man is in the Nelson-Atkins Museum, Kansas City, and another is in the Société Historique et Littéraire Polonaise, Paris. The entire group is discussed and reproduced in the monographic exhibition devoted to the artist (Nice and elsewhere 1977, nos. 404–9, repr.). Four of the portraits were once in the Goncourt collection, and Edmond wrote that the artist, contrary to his usual manner, "a été sauvé de la convention, et forcé pour ainsi dire d'être français par l'étude rigoureuse de la nature."

In his time, van Loo became the most famous of a family of painters of Flemish descent who worked in France. His particular facility for drawing won him first prize at the Académie Royale in 1723, when he was only eighteen. Beginning his studies in Paris, he completed them in Italy and returned to France in 1734. Elected to the Académie in 1735 and appointed *premier peintre du roi* in 1762, he became director of the Académie in 1763. Van Loo was recognized by his contemporaries, not only those in France but elsewhere on the Continent, as the first painter of Europe. While his portraits of the king and queen are at Versailles, his many other works are located in museums throughout the world. Although his reputation as a painter has diminished over time, he is still recognized for his fine draughtsmanship, especially for his work in chalk, which demonstrates his dexterity of handling and deft rendering of forms. The present example is no exception. Such details as the sitter's dress and cap, along with her easy and natural pose, attest to van Loo's skill. CDD

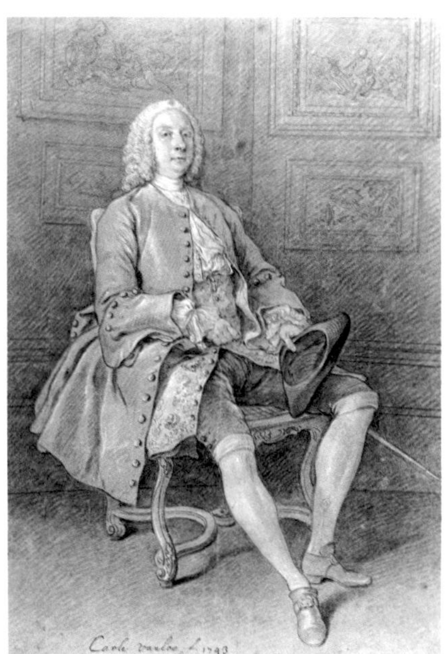

Fig. 1 Carle van Loo, *Portrait of a Seated Man*, The Pierpont Morgan Library, 1971.11.

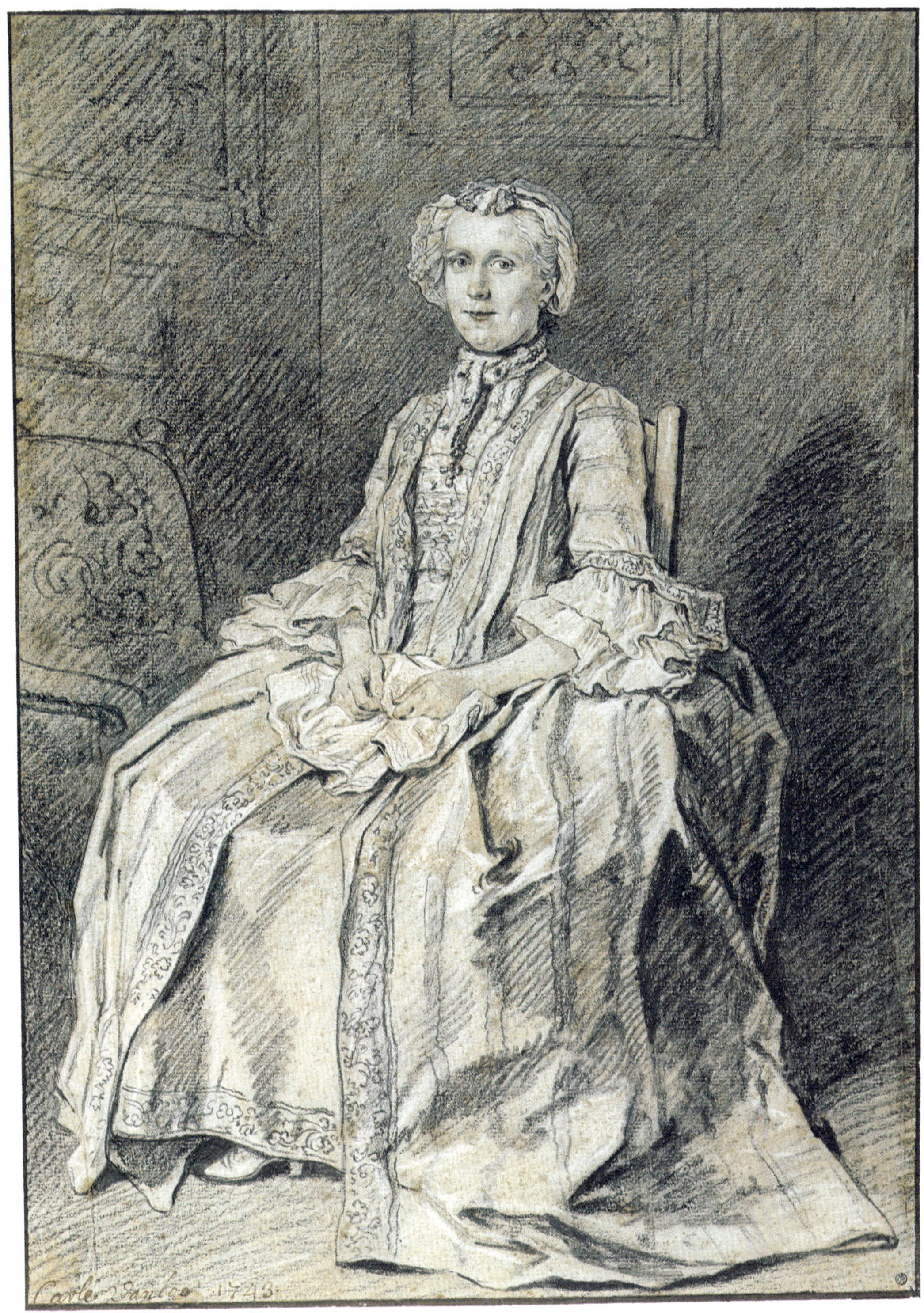
Carle Vanloo 1743

9

JEAN-BAPTISTE PERRONNEAU

Paris 1715–1783 Amsterdam

Portrait of a Man, 1756

Pastel. 21 3/4 x 17 1/2 inches (550 x 440 mm). Watermark: none visible through lining. Signed at upper right in graphite, *Perronneau*; inscribed on verso, *Juillet 1756, par Perroneau.*

PROVENANCE: Sigismond Bardac; his sale, Paris, 10–11 May 1920, no. 30, repr. (25,500 frs.); Jacques Stern; sale, Paris, Hôtel Drouot, 3 April 1979, lot 41 (where it is suggested that the sitter may be Jacques Cazotte [Etude Laurin-Guillaume-Buffetard-Tailleur]); David Carritt Limited, London.

BIBLIOGRAPHY: Vaillat and Ratouis 1923, p. 218; New York PML 1984, no. 57; PML/*FR* XXI, 1989, p. 368.

1984.6

Perronneau, whose ability as a portraitist was particularly appreciated within the artistic community, painted or executed in pastels the likenesses of a number of contemporary artists, including his rival, Quentin de La Tour. Seven of his best, among them portraits of Laurent Cars (1699–1771) and Gabriel Huquier (1695–1772), are preserved in the Louvre's Cabinet des dessins (repr. Geneviève Monnier, *Pastels XVIIème et XVIIIème siècles*, Paris, 1972, nos. 91–96). Perronneau was apprenticed to the printmaker Cars and continued his studies with Natoire and Drouais. The especially strong portrait of Huquier is one of the earliest known examples of Perronneau's pastels. The artist's commissions often took him out of Paris—to Orléans, Toulouse, and Lyons—and even to Italy, Russia, Hungary, Poland, as well as to Holland, where the finesse of his portraiture was much appreciated.

It has been suggested that the handsome subject of this portrait is Jacques Cazotte (1719–1792). While this identification cannot be positively confirmed, it is doubtless based on the sitter's strong resemblance to Cazotte in his oil portrait by Perronneau, in the National Gallery, London (repr. *Gazette des Beaux Arts* 89 [March 1977], suppl. p. 68, fig. 291). Educated by the Jesuits, Cazotte showed an early aptitude for writing poetry. However, at age twenty-seven, he was sent to Martinique as marine controller of the Windward Islands. He continued to write in his spare time until he was able to devote himself full-time to this pursuit in his early forties. He then produced a number of works, including his prose poem, *Olivier*, and *Diable amoureux*, *Guerre civile de Genève*, *La Brunette anglaise*, and even the libretto for an opéra comique production. A lifelong royalist, he was executed in 1792. In what seems an almost apocryphal note, he is credited with having said, "Je meurs comme j'ai vécu, fidèle à Dieu et à mon roi."

The portrait is still in its original carved gilt frame, surmounted by a pair of quills bound by laurel leaves—presumably an allusion to the literary avocation of the sitter, whether he be Cazotte or another writer. CDD

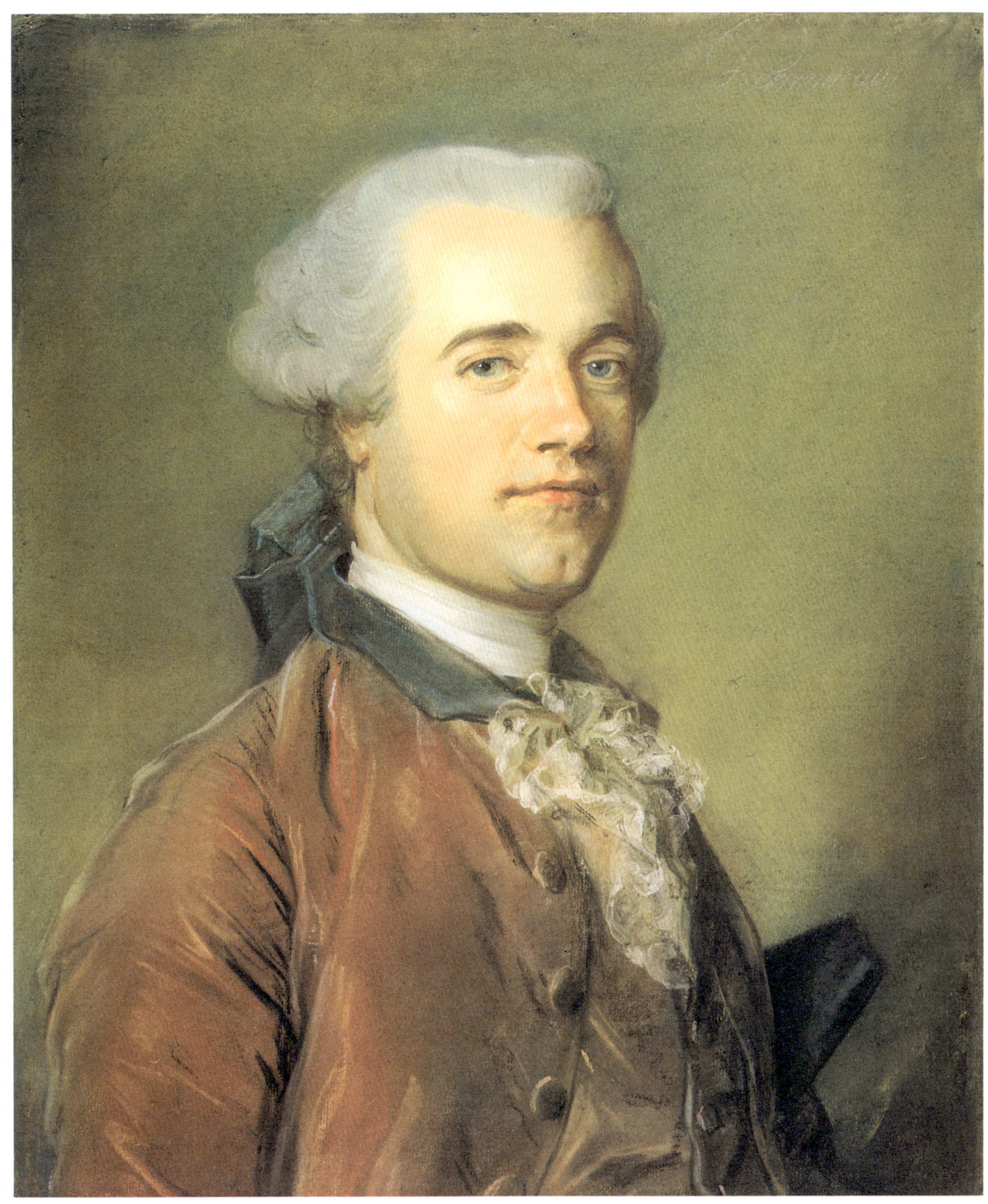

10

JEAN-BAPTISTE LALLEMAND

Dijon 1716–1803 Paris

Imaginary Landscape with Castle and a Small Cascade on a River

Gouache, over preliminary indications in graphite. 10 1/4 x 16 3/8 inches (260 x 417 mm). Watermark: none visible through lining. Signed at lower right, in pen and white ink, *lallemand*; numbered on back of old mount, in pen and brown ink, *No 13*.

PROVENANCE: Adolphe Stoll, Paris (Lugt 2786c); private collection, Massachusetts; E. V. Thaw & Co., Inc., New York.

BIBLIOGRAPHY: PML/*FR* XX, 1984, pp. 269–70.

1982.3

Although Jean-Baptiste Lallemand never achieved the fame and prominence of his contemporary, the marine landscape painter Joseph Vernet (1714–1789), this brilliantly colored gouache of an imaginary landscape, perhaps inspired by the artist's native Burgundy, attests to his mastery in creating idyllic views of the French countryside.

With the notable exception of Pierre Quarré's introduction to the catalogue of the 1954 exhibition of Lallemand's drawings and paintings at the museum in Dijon, little information concerning the artist's life and oeuvre has been published. The son of a tailor in Dijon, Lallemand was trained in his father's métier but used his leisure time to draw and paint. He came to Paris, hoping to be employed in a tailor's shop, but instead found a patron for his paintings *The Four Seasons* and, in 1745, at age twenty-nine, was accepted at the Académie de St. Luc in Paris. Soon thereafter, he departed for Italy to study, settled in Rome, married, and enjoyed considerable success, not returning to France until 1761. A group of his drawings of Rome and the Campagna, originally acquired by the seventh earl of Elgin in 1799, was exhibited at Agnew's in London in October 1963. Lallemand exhibited at the Academy in Paris in 1751 and 1764 as well as in several later shows (1776, 1783, and 1786). He also worked for some time in England (a *Still Life* is mentioned in the 1773 records of the Society of Artists). Most important and impressive, however, in sheer numbers are his ninety-nine drawings (views of the Franche-Comté, Bourgogne, Lyonnais, etc.) used as illustrations to Volume V of *Description générale et particulière ou Voyage pittoresque de la France*, Paris, 1781 (figs. 1 and 2). This magnum opus, commissioned by Jean Benjamin de Laborde and others, was to consist of twelve volumes but was never completed (the set at the Bibliothèque Nationale comprises eight volumes). Lallemand's designs, which often were made on the spot (*dessiné d'après nature*), were transferred to the plate by many well-known engravers, most of them by or under the direction of François Denis Née (1732–1817).

This landscape reflects Lallemand's intimate relationship with Burgundy and the Franche-Comté. Certain elements of the composition—such as the round tower, the cattle, the shepherdess on horseback, the waterfall, and the trees bending in a gentle breeze—were observed by the artist while sketching sites intended for the *Voyage pittoresque* and combined in this pastoral fantasy. This drawing's affinity with the landscapes of the *Voyage pittoresque* suggests a date between 1771 and 1781. Gouache was a very popular medium at this period in France, its colors being well suited to the luxurious interiors of the rococo. RSK

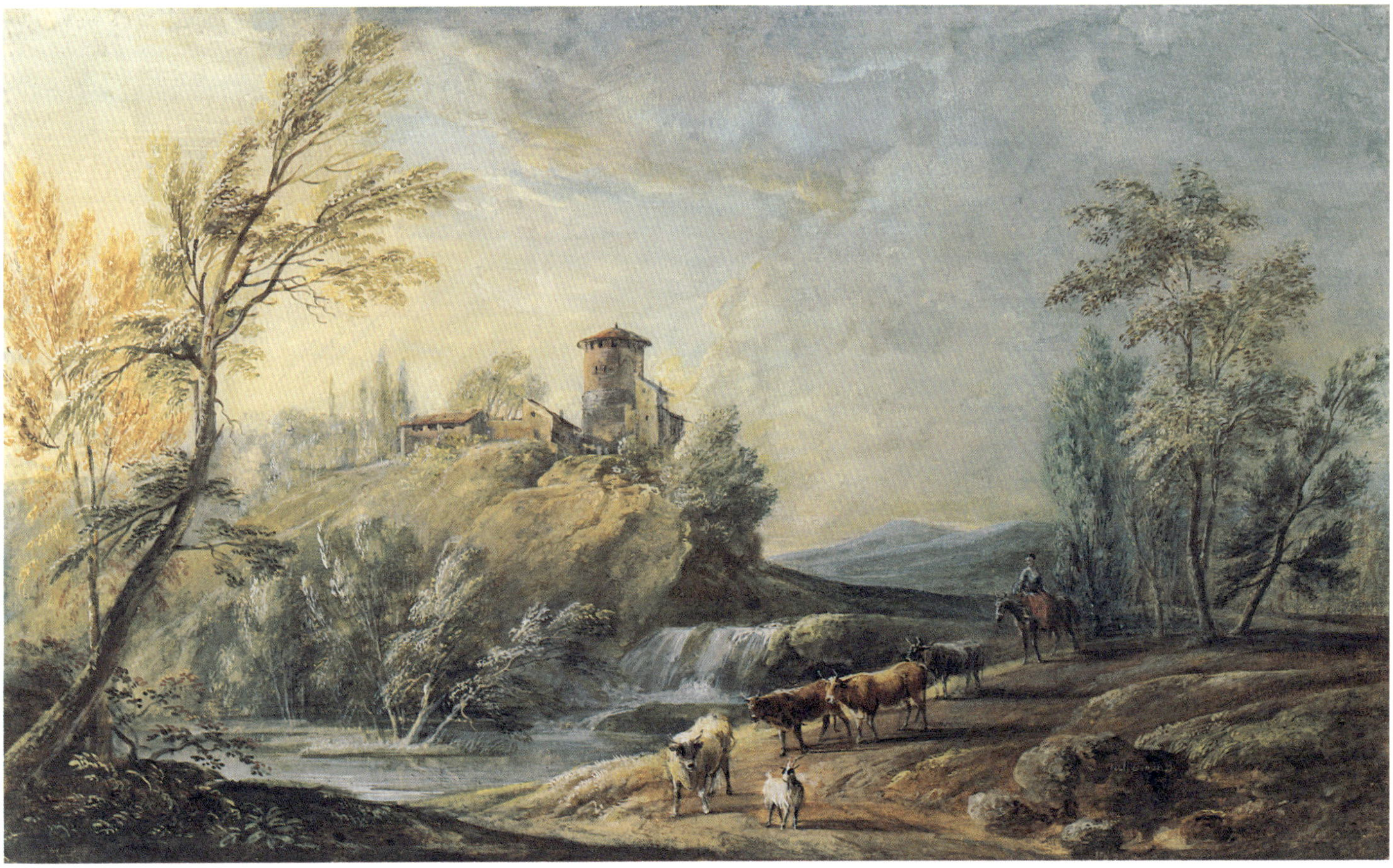

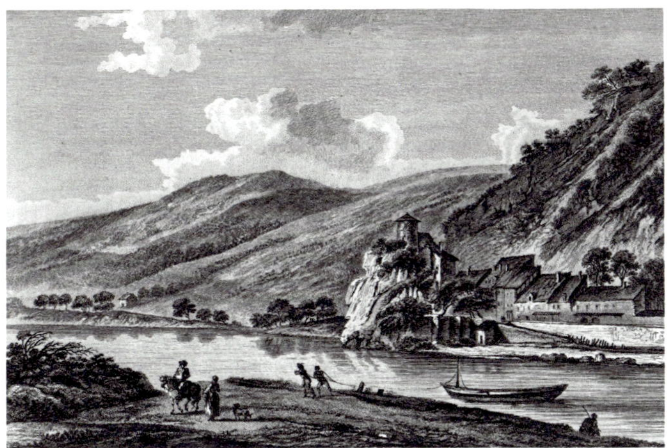

Fig. 1 Jean-Baptiste Lallemand, *View of the Porte Taillée, Besançon* in *Voyage pittoresque de la France* (vol. V, no. 3), General Research Division, The New York Public Library, Astor, Lenox and Tilden Foundations.

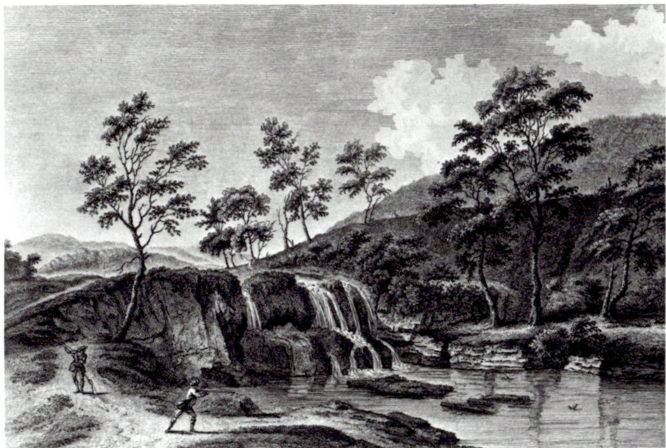

Fig. 2 Jean-Baptiste Lallemand, *View of a Waterfall*, in *Voyage pittoresque de la France* (vol. V, no. 22), General Research Division, The New York Public Library, Astor, Lenox and Tilden Foundations.

11

LOUIS CARROGIS, called CARMONTELLE

Paris 1717–1806 Paris

Portrait of Mme de Sireuil Seated in a Landscape

Watercolor over black and red chalk, laid down on mount decorated with pale green border. 11 1/4 x 7 1/8 inches (285 x 182 mm). Watermark: none visible through lining.

PROVENANCE: Mme de Sireuil; by descent in the Sireuil family; Albert Meyer, Paris; sale, London, Sotheby's, 23 March 1972, lot 72, repr.; Galerie Cailleux; private collection, Paris; Galerie de Bayser, Paris.

BIBLIOGRAPHY: Ricci 1935, no. 19, repr.

EXHIBITIONS: Paris 1933, no. 31; Paris 1935, no. 20.

1992.3

Not much is known about Carmontelle's early life or training. The son of a Parisian shoemaker, he eventually was engaged to tutor the duc de Chartres, son of the duc d'Orléans, in mathematics. Both father and son came to appreciate Carmontelle's many other capabilities. Skilled as a painter, engraver, architect, dramatist, comedian, and organizer of festivals, Carmontelle also designed the Parc Monceau in Paris. By the end of his life, he would produce more than 750 portraits, filling eleven albums. He confided the names of most of his sitters to an old friend, Richard de Lédans, who set them down in a manuscript list now at Chantilly. After Carmontelle's death, Lédans unsuccessfully attempted to sell all the portrait albums en bloc, first to the Bibliothèque Imperiale and then to Talleyrand. He eventually gave some of the portraits to relatives of the sitters and sold others. After his death, some 520 of the portraits were purchased by Pierre de La Mésangère (1761–1831), supposedly the person who placed them on the familiar green mounts still being used and annotated each with its sitter's name, transcribed from the manuscript. Eventually 440 of these portraits in albums were sold to the grandson of the duc de Chartres, the duc d'Aumale, who reorganized the collection, breaking up the chronological order of the original albums. Subsequently he added many other portraits to the collection at Chantilly, which now numbers 570.

Mostly executed in profile, Carmontelle's portraits have considerable charm and quite effectively capture the mannerisms and appearance of the sitter. The artist would first make a rapid full-length sketch in trois crayons, later adding watercolor and gouache to complete the portrait.

The portrait of Mme de Sireuil, however, along with the companion drawing of M. de Sireuil, was not annotated, since the drawing was in the Sireuil family until the twentieth century (presumably Carmontelle gave the drawing to the Sireuils). Ennobled in 1715, the Sireuils come from Anjou and the Touraine. The Mme de Sireuil represented here is likely the wife of the collector, whose extensive drawings collection was sold over the course of several days in December 1781. A very cultivated man, interested in both literature and the arts, and a friend of Boucher, M. de Sireuil had such a great passion for the artist's work that he acquired a very large collection of drawings of every type as well as some paintings (see No. 5).

Mme de Sireuil is quite whimsically depicted here, seated in a chair in her garden with a rather imposing porticoed house lightly sketched in the background. She wears a laced-trimmed bright red dressing gown and black bonnet, which is tied under her chin. Gazing through spectacles, she appears to be admiring a posy she holds in her upraised right hand. CDD

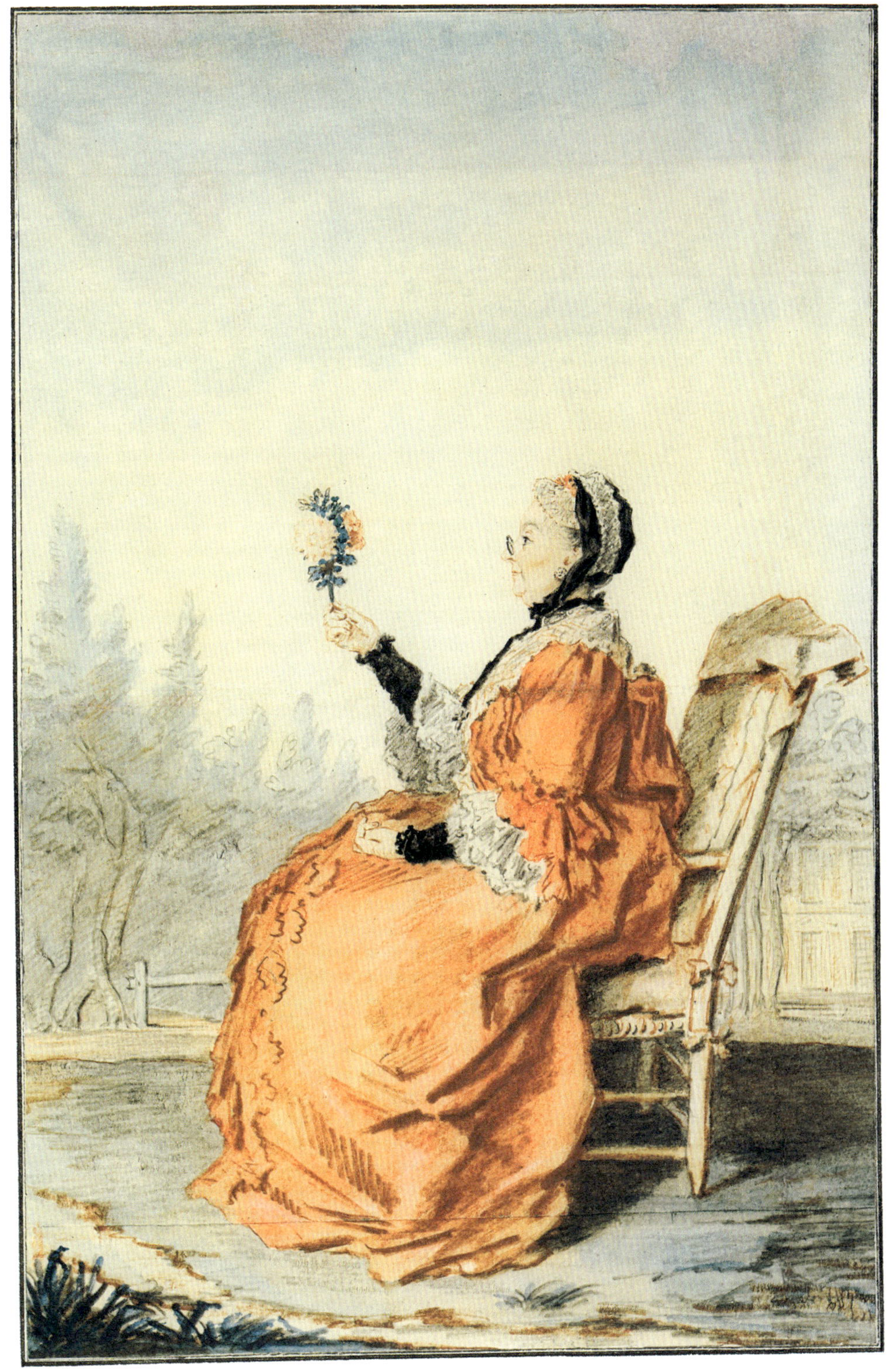

31

12

GABRIEL DE SAINT-AUBIN

Paris 1724–1780 Paris

The Lesson of the Chemist Sage at the Hôtel des Monnaies, 1779

Black chalk with some stumping and graphite, point of brush and brown ink, gray wash, some bodycolor. 7 7/8 x 5 1/16 inches (198 x 128 mm). Watermark: fragment of crown. Signed and dated at lower margin, in pen and black ink, *par Gabriel St. Aubin 1779*; in graphite, *La leçon de M. Sage a l'hotel de la Monaye*.

PROVENANCE: Jacques Doucet, Paris; his sale, Galerie Georges Petit, Paris, 5 June 1912, vol. I, lot 54, no. 50, repr.; G. Pardinel (30,200 frs.); François Coty, Paris; sale, Galerie Jean Charpentier, Paris, 30 November–1 December 1936, lot 15, repr.; Samuel Kress, New York; Mrs. Kilvert, New York; Audrey Cory de Ayala, New York and Paris; Mr. and Mrs. Robert H. Smith, Bethesda, Md.; Rosenberg & Stiebel, New York.

BIBLIOGRAPHY: Dilke 1902, p. 134, repr. opp. p. 134; Tourneux 1904, p. 28, repr.; Dacier 1911; Dacier 1929–31, II, no. 435; Paris 1984, under no. 3.

EXHIBITIONS: Paris 1925, no. 81; Ann Arbor 1969, no. 69; Middletown and Baltimore 1975, no. 57, repr.; Paris and New York 1993–94, no. 64, repr.

1991.4

On 11 June 1778, Balthasar Georges Sage (1740–1824) was appointed to the newly created chair of domestic mineralogy and metallurgy at the Hôtel des Monnaies. At the age of nineteen, Sage inspired the confidence of several rich patrons who advanced him 30,000 francs to establish a chemistry lab and a mineralogy collection. By 1778 Sage had become a member of the Académie des sciences. Saint-Aubin's drawing, made just a year after this appointment, depicts the well-known chemist in the midst of a lesson. Sage's experiments and published works at this time, including *Art d'imiter les pierres précieuses* (1778) and *Art d'essayer l'or et l'argent* (1780), dealt with precious stones and metals. In 1783 the Ecole des mines was founded at Sage's instigation, and he was named director.

The Hôtel des Monnaies had been established on the rue de la Monnaie at the beginning of the fourteenth century. In 1768 Louis XV ordered the demolition of the hôtel, and that year Jacques Denis Antoine was commissioned to design a new building, which was completed in 1777. The new hôtel attracted the attention of many artists because of the "harmonie de ses proportions et la magnificence de l'ensemble." This is one of three known drawings by Saint-Aubin recording Sage's lectures and demonstrations, one of which is in the Musée Carnavalet (Dacier 1929–31, II, nos. 435–37). It is one of six drawings by Saint-Aubin in the Library and is in many ways the most typical by the artist, who is especially well known for his brilliant and highly journalistic works recording Parisian contemporary life.

CDD

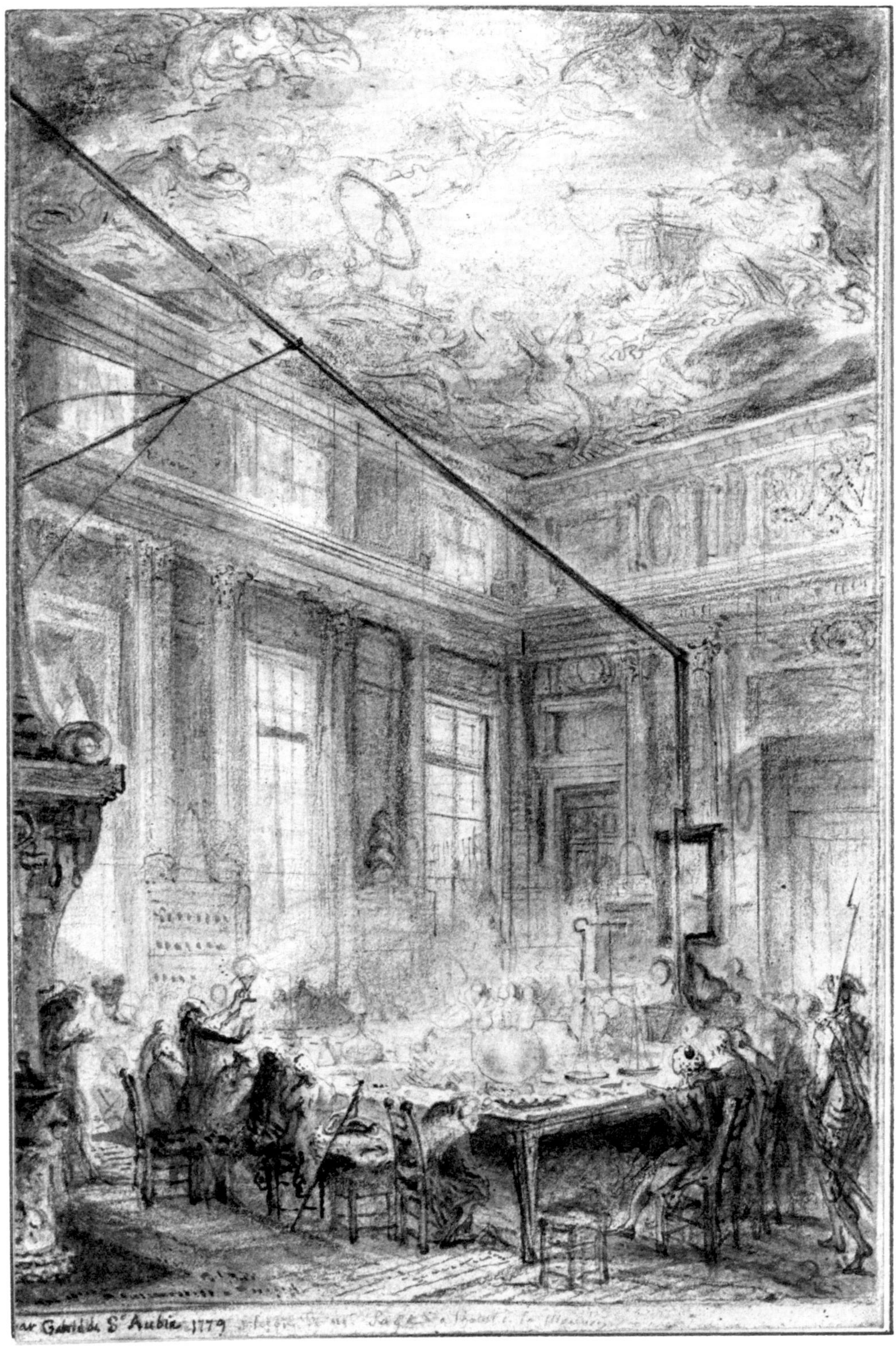

13

GABRIEL DE SAINT-AUBIN

Paris 1724–1780 Paris

Young Woman Standing on the Seat of a Carriage

Black chalk, with touches of black ink and gray wash. 6 1/2 x 8 15/16 inches (166 x 226 mm). Watermark: fragment of a coat of arms surmounted by a crown within a circle. Inscribed on verso at lower center in graphite, *dessin J.*(?)*S Aubin acheté à* [illegible].

PROVENANCE: Baron Jérôme Pichon; his sale, Paris, 17 May 1897, lot 130 (as *Mlle Duthé aux Champs Elysées* [55 frs. with lot 129]); Henri Pannier; his sale, Paris, 9 May 1919, lot 39 (2,000 frs.); Paul Helleu; his sale, Paris, 28–29 March 1928, lot 84, repr. (13,100 frs.); F. Koenigs, Haarlem; M. and Mme Boerlage-Koenigs, Laren; Artemis Fine Arts, London.

BIBLIOGRAPHY: Dacier 1929–31, II, no. 722; PML/*FR* XXI, 1989, p. 337.

EXHIBITIONS: Paris and Amsterdam 1964, no. 85, pl. 103; New York PML 1984, no. 65; Paris and New York 1993–94, no. 63, repr.

1984.7

Almost a hundred years ago, this subject was identified as Mlle Duthé on the Champs Elysées. It was thought to reflect Saint-Aubin's interest in the episode, recorded in the *Mémoires secrets* of the famous courtesan, in which she called attention to herself by standing on top of her carriage in the manner of a lady of quality at the Champs Elysées until an outraged crowd drove her away (Pichon sale catalogue, under lot 130). This picturesque interpretation has not been considered viable for some time, and it seems likely that Saint-Aubin simply made a sketch of this young lady on the spot, having seen her standing outside her carriage with her coachman and footmen, probably in order to get a better view of a royal entry or some other ceremonial activity. That the young woman is the real subject of the drawing is borne out by her detailed treatment as opposed to the sketchy delineation of her servants and horses. CDD

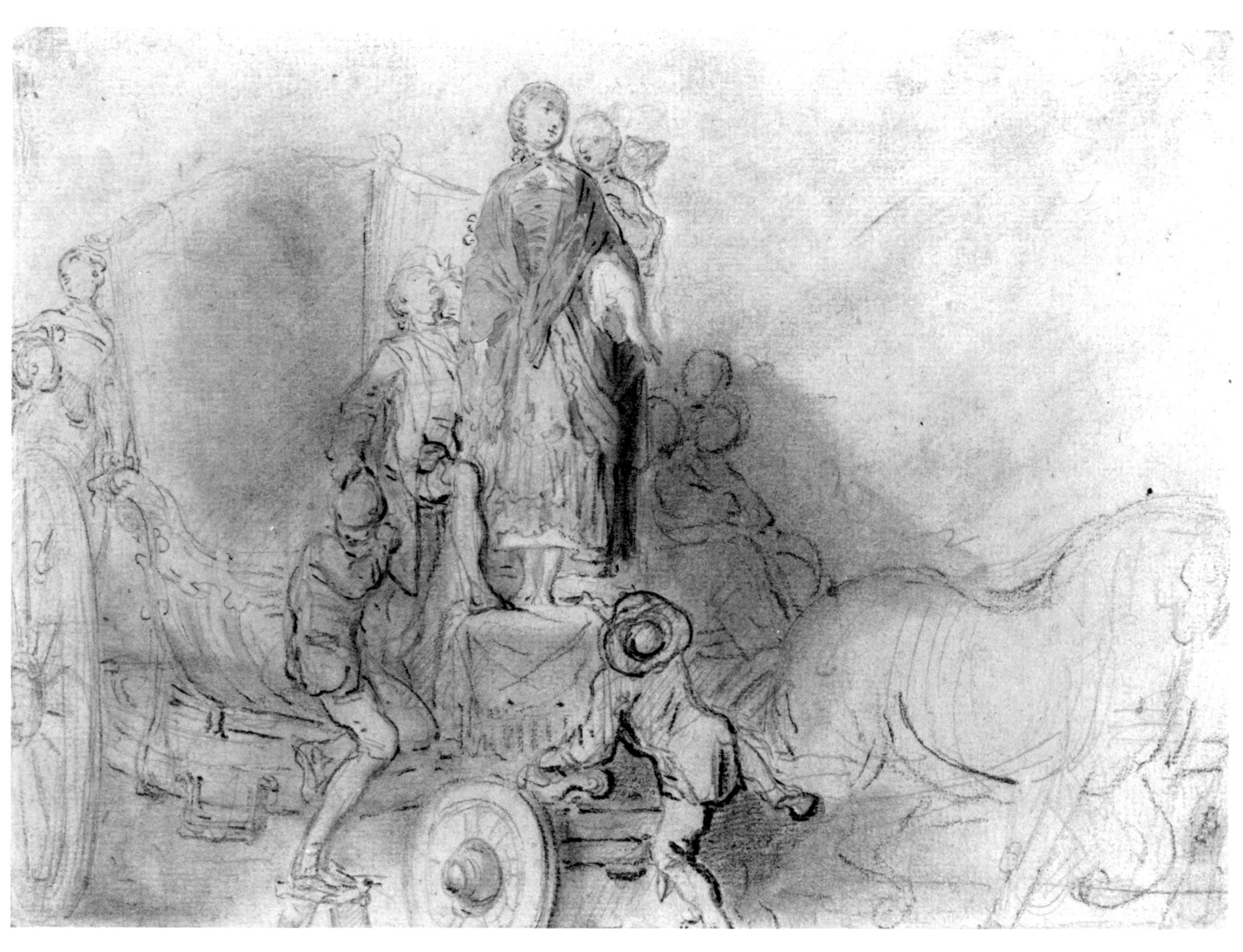

14

FRANÇOIS-HUBERT DROUAIS

Paris 1727–1775 Paris

Boy with a Sketchbook

Black, white, and red chalk. 10 x 16 inches (256 x 404 mm). Watermark: crown with fleur-de-lis and unidentified figures. Inscribed on the old mount, *F. H. Drouais.*

PROVENANCE: Thomas Williams, London; W. M. Brady, New York.

1992.35

The subject of a boy carrying a portfolio occurs frequently in the oeuvre of this well-known portraitist. A similar drawing, the subject of which was identified as Drouais's son and apprentice, was exhibited in Amsterdam in 1930. A painted version (sale, London, Phillips, 11 December 1990, no. 271, repr.), which may be identical with the painting once owned by the marquis de Marigny, was engraved by Damman and translated into a tapestry by Cozette. That these works are all signed and dated 1760 dispels the attractive notion that the boy represented is the artist's son. Drouais was married only two years earlier, in 1758, the year that he became *peintre du roi.* The painting in the Marigny collection, sold in 1781, lot 36, was once described as a portrait of the duc de Choiseul: "d'apres M. Prosper Dorbec, qui a consacré une judicieuse étude aux Drouais, ce portrait ne saurait être celui du duc de Choiseul, neveu du ministre de Louis XV," because "l'âge du personnage répresenté . . . ne concordent pas avec celui qu'avait à cette époque le jeune duc de Choiseul, c'est à dire Claude-Antoine-Gabriel de Choiseul, neveu du ministre de Louis XV, lequel était né en 1760."

François-Hubert was the best known of the three generations of artists bearing the Drouais name. At the time Mariette compiled his *Abecedario,* he wrote, "il se distingue dans le genre du portrait et est en vogue." Drouais's success had begun with the Salon of 1755, where he exhibited, among other works, the portrait of a little boy titled *Le Petit Polisson.* Almost immediately thereafter, he found favor at court, and in 1757 his double portrait of the infant sons of the dauphin, the future Louis XVI and Louis XVIII, ensured his success as a portraitist, particularly of children. Drouais became *premier peintre* in 1772. CDD

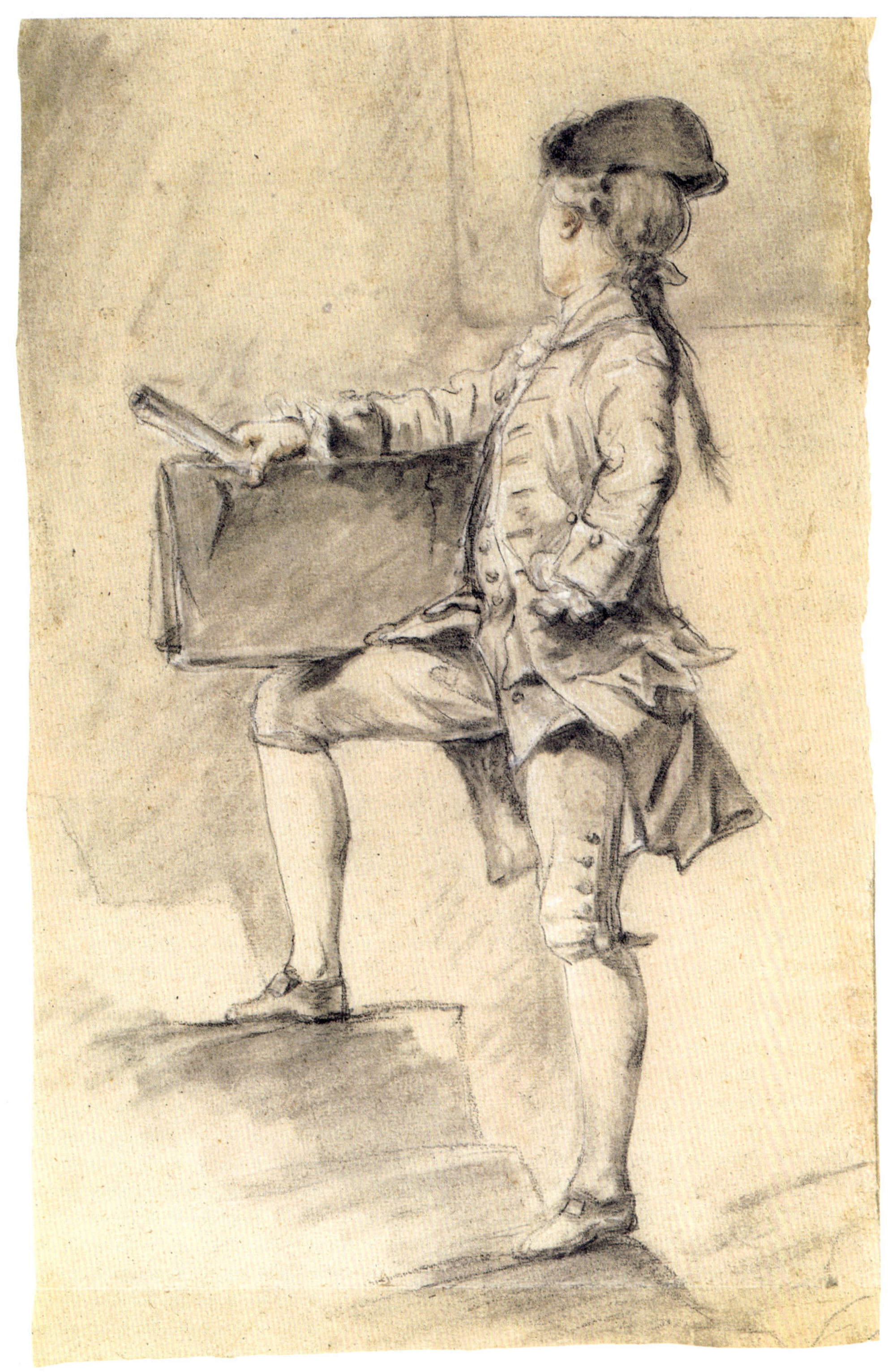

15

JEAN HONORE FRAGONARD

Grasse 1732–1806 Paris

Seated Young Woman

Red chalk. 13 3/8 x 9 inches (340 x 229 mm). Watermark: pot (close to Heawood 3695).

PROVENANCE: possibly François Renaud (Lugt 1042); Edmond Filleul; Galerie de Bayser, Paris.

1993.6

For many years this drawing was known only by the attractive counterproof reworked by the artist, now in the Fine Arts Museums of San Francisco (fig. 1). The pensive young model appears to be the artist's daughter, Rosalie, familiar from several studies Fragonard made of her during the 1780s. Rosalie and Fragonard's appealing sister-in-law, Marguerite Gérard, sat for many of the artist's drawings at this time, and it is a matter of speculation as to which young woman provided the inspiration for such drawings as *A Young Woman Seated* (Paris and New York 1993–94, no. 69, repr. [in color]).

It is certainly Rosalie, however, who appears in the series of ravishing red chalk drawings to which this example relates. These continue throughout the 1780s until her death from consumption in October of 1788 at only eighteen years of age. One of the earliest, now in the Rijksmuseum, Amsterdam, shows her standing, aged thirteen or fourteen, wearing a pretty, long silk dress (Massengale 1993, pl. 40, p. 125). As has been noted elsewhere, Fragonard began making occasional counterproofs of his red chalk drawings when he was a student at the French Academy in Rome, frequently reworking them to very different effect. The San Francisco counterproof of this drawing is a good example of this practice. Fragonard added the parrot and accented the counterproof with brown wash.

The way in which Rosalie sits, holding a pillow, suggests that she may be tired, perhaps already ill. She is also depicted, in an advanced stage of illness, in a similar drawing that was in the collection of J. P. Heseltine (Ananoff 1961, no. 182; Massengale 1993, fig. 68). In that drawing, she wears a morning gown and looks directly ahead, her eyes large and shadowed. A pillow supports her, and beside her is a basin on a low chest.

CDD

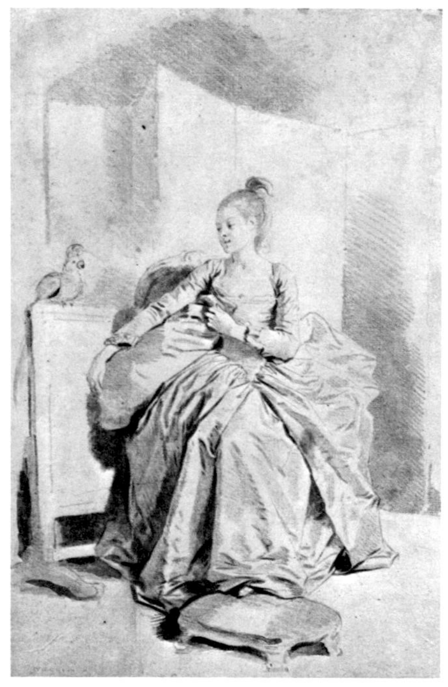

Fig. 1 Jean Honoré Fragonard, *Woman with a Parrot*, Achenbach Foundation for Graphic Arts, Fine Arts Museums of San Francisco, 1966.54.

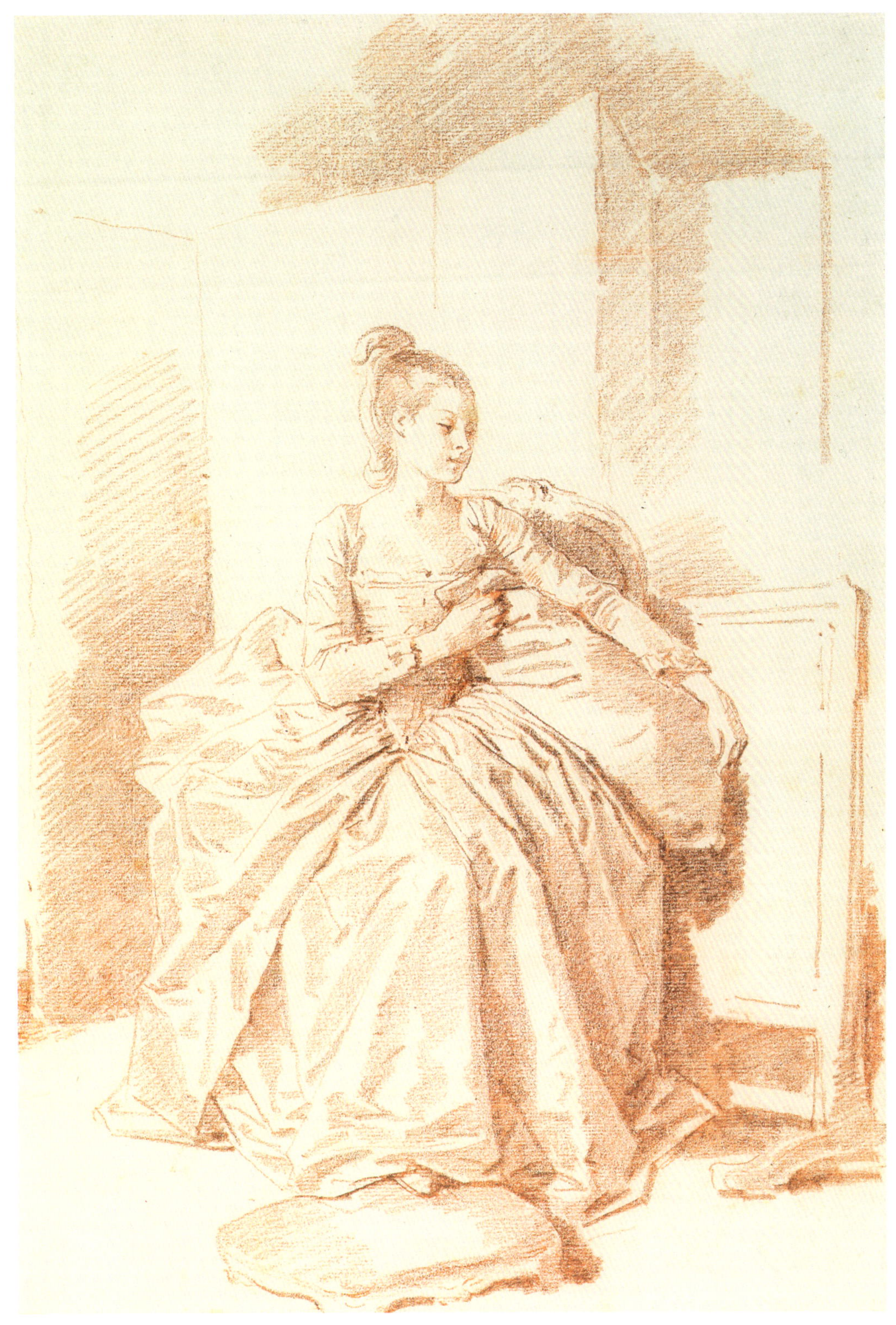

39

16

HUBERT ROBERT

Paris 1733–1808 Paris

View of the Temple of Neptune and the Basilica at Paestum, 1760

Red chalk. 13 5/16 x 19 1/2 inches (340 x 483 mm). Watermark: fleur-de-lis within a circle, surmounted by a crown. Signed at lower left, in red chalk, *Roberti 1760*; inscribed at lower center, possibly by the artist, in pen and brown ink, *vue d'est* (?) *des Temples de*, and in a different ink, *a* (superimposed over the *de*) *pestum* and *Roberti f*(?) (effaced).

PROVENANCE: Adolphe Stein, Paris.

BIBLIOGRAPHY: PML/*FR* XX, 1984, p. 294.

EXHIBITIONS: New York PML 1989; Montreal 1993, no. 102, repr.

1982.103

This drawing is close enough to Robert's view of Paestum in the *Voyage pittoresque* (fig. 1) to be counted as one of his preparations for the plate. Here, the figural group in the foreground is different, as is the temple, viewed from an angle showing more of the side. Saint-Non eventually chose a drawing (now in the Musée des Beaux-Arts, Rouen) with a more frontal view of the temple as the basis for the print in the *Voyage pittoresque* (repr. Rome, Villa Medici, *J. H. Fragonard e H. Robert a Roma*, catalogue by Jean-Pierre Cuzin, Pierre Rosenberg, and Catherine Bulot, 1990–91, no. 44).

The drawings Robert made at Paestum were highly praised by Mariette in his *Abecedario*: "M. l'abbé de Saint-Non l'a beaucoup fait travailler dans le temps qu'il étoit à Rome, en 1760 et 1761, et lui a fait faire le voyage de Naples. Il en a profité pour dessiner sur le lieu les fameuses antiquités de Pestum, qu'il a parfaitement rendues." A number of drawings, all of a size similar to this one, survive, including one view known only through its counterproof, which is preserved in the Bibliothèque Municipale, Besançon, and *View of the Temple at Paestum*, which was on the art market in 1969 (Paris, Hôtel Drouot, 26 November 1969, no. 17 A, repr.; 330 x 440 mm). The latter is extremely close to the present drawing, although the temple is seen from a less frontal viewpoint. The tree that overarches the temple and the treatment of the sky differ, but the reed hut and staffage figures are much the same. A larger drawing (380 x 550 mm), in which the temple is surrounded with water, is in the Pushkin Museum, Moscow. The nearly identical views of the temple and basilica in the Morgan and Rouen drawings, along with the similar depictions of the darkly mottled clouds that Robert used as accents in a wide expanse of sky, make it likely that both drawings were executed on the same day. Robert's great facility as a draughtsman of ruins was praised by Saint-Non in his journal: "J'avois emmené avec moy Robert jeune Peintre de la plus grande Espérance et du premier Talent dans le genre de l'Architecture et des Ruînes." CDD

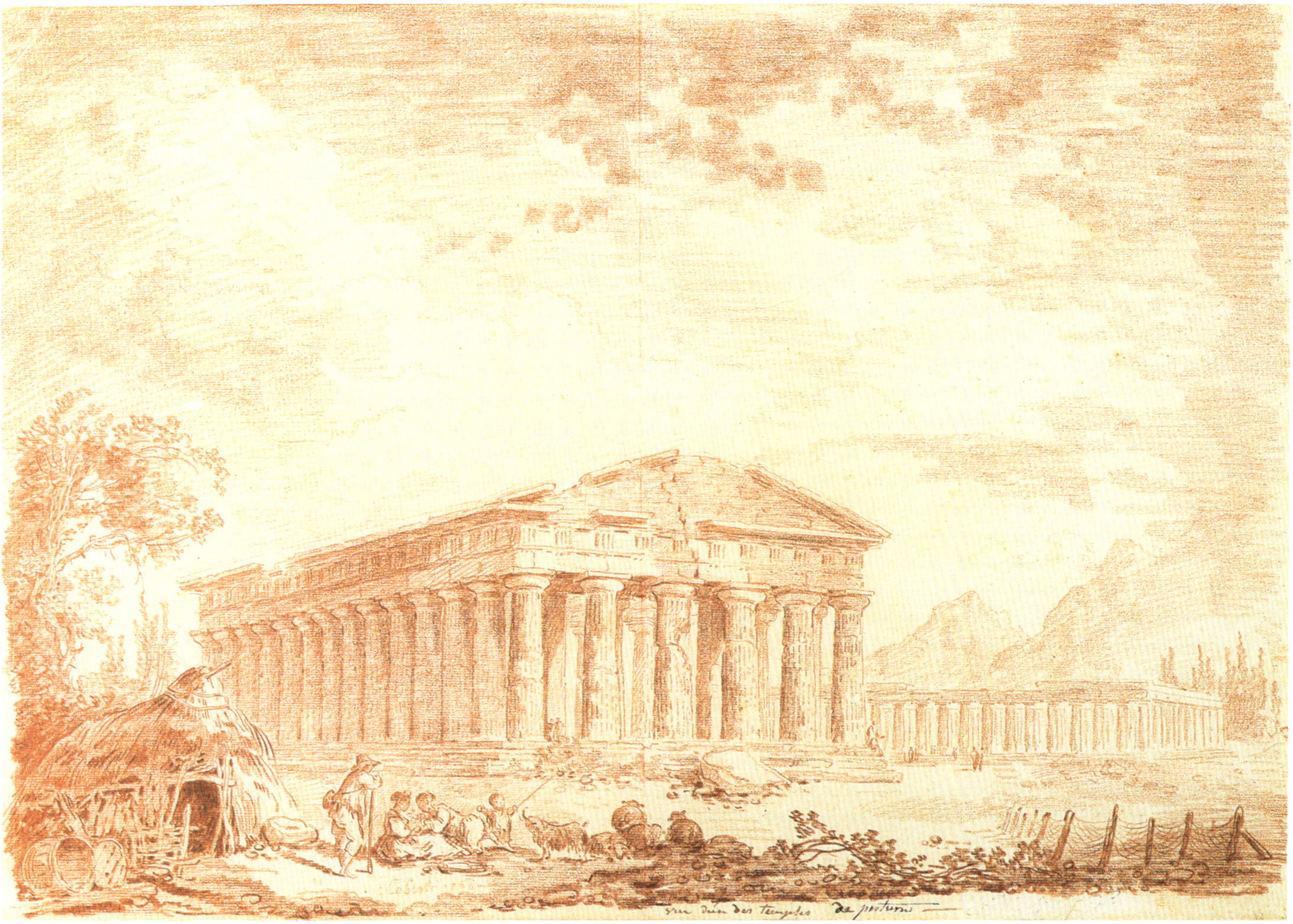

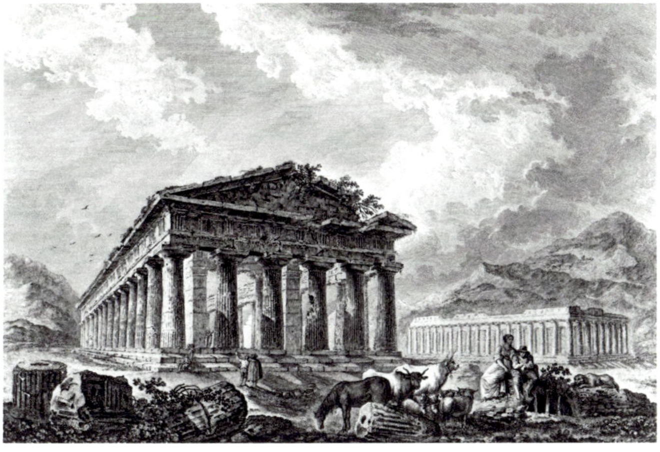

Fig. 1 Hubert Robert, *View of Paestum*, in *Voyage pittoresque* (vol. III, opposite p. 157), The Pierpont Morgan Library, PML 62643++.

17

JEAN PIERRE LAURENT HOUEL

Rouen 1735–1813 Paris

Rocky Landscape with a Waterfall and Fishermen

Gouache and point of brush. 15 3/16 x 20 1/2 inches (386 x 520 mm). Watermark: fragment of a coat of arms, letter *T* on a globe (cf. Heawood 2394).

PROVENANCE: Galerie Cailleux, Paris.

EXHIBITION: Paris and New York 1993–94, no. 80, repr.

1992.9

Hoüel, who studied with Jean-Baptiste Descamps and later, in Paris, with Lebas and Casanova, was a proficient engraver and landscape painter. While he is known for the engravings he made after a series of drawings by Boucher, it was the series of landscapes he painted for the duc de Choiseul's château at Chanteloup that brought him the most attention and earned him sufficient recognition to receive lodgings, if not a *pensionnaire*'s place, at the French Academy in Rome. Mariette tells us in his *Abecedario*, "il a trouvé à Rome des Anglois *[sic]* qui lui ont fait faire le voyage de Naples, et d'autres qui tout de suite l'ont conduit en Sicile, et, dans ces contrées, il a fait, à ce que j'entends, quantité d'études qui servirent à améliorer sa manière qui est agréable, et qui rend assez parfaitement les effets de la nature. Car c'est au genre de paysage qu'il s'est consacré." Hoüel traveled extensively in Italy on two trips and brought back numerous watercolors and gouaches. A series of forty-six gouache drawings made in connection with his trip to Sicily between 1776 and 1779 was the subject of a recent exhibition at the Louvre (*Hoüel: voyage en Sicile 1776–1779*, 1990). The drawings were part of the extensive preparations for his own version of a *Voyage pittoresque* to Sicily, a project he had conceived while in the company of Watelet.

While Italianate in character, the mise-en-scène of the present drawing is not sufficiently specific to be identifiable, and it seems most likely that the landscape was inspired by Italy rather than based on a real view. Indeed, the spontaneity and naturalism of this rendering is not unlike that of the work of Moreau l'Aîné (No. 18). As Marianne Roland Michel observed, the treatment of the shadows and stormy sky is reminiscent of a painting of the Castle of Saint-Ouen-les-Vignes, now in the Musée de Tours, that the artist executed for the duc de Choiseul at Chanteloup. Hoüel's subject matter and treatment of the sky are typical of his work in the late 1780s. CDD

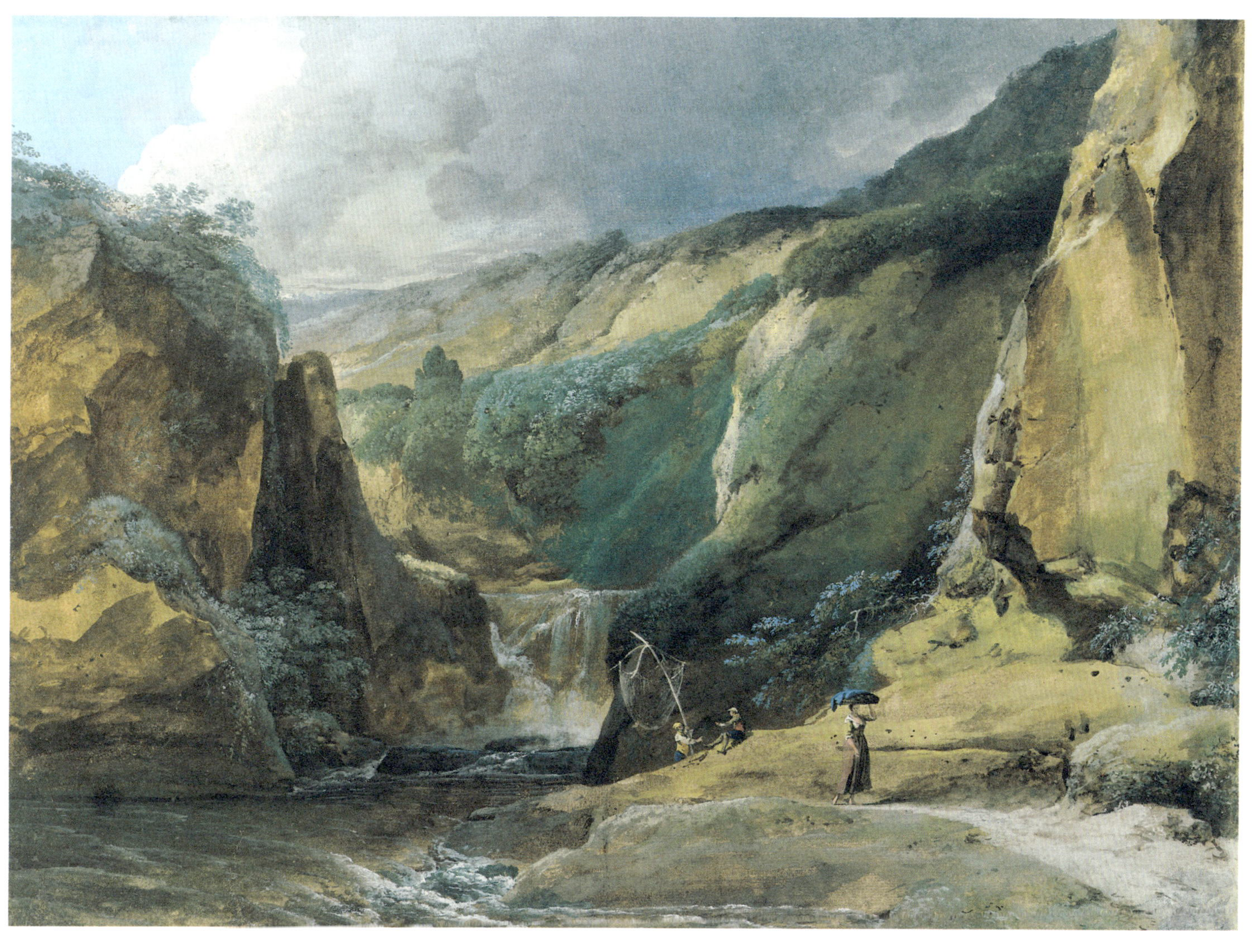

18

LOUIS GABRIEL MOREAU, called L'AINE

Paris 1740–1806 Paris

La Vallée: Pastoral River Landscape

Gouache over preliminary indications in graphite. 22 7/8 x 33 5/16 inches (593 x 844 mm). Watermark: none visible through lining. Signed with initials at lower left, in pen and black ink, *L M.*

PROVENANCE: David David-Weill, Neuilly; Mme Jacques Balsan (née Consuelo Vanderbilt, duchess of Marlborough); E. V. Thaw & Co., Inc., New York.

BIBLIOGRAPHY: Wildenstein 1923, p. 69, no. 180, pl. 180; Henriot 1927, p. 125, repr.; PML/*FR* XX, 1984, p. 279; Michel 1987, p. 42, fig. 30 (in color).

EXHIBITIONS: Baltimore 1941, no. 64, pl. 62, repr.; New York PML 1984, no. 82; Paris and New York 1993–94, no. 84, repr. (in color).

1981.11

Louis Gabriel Moreau, called l'Aîné to distinguish him from his brother, the book illustrator Jean-Michel Moreau, le Jeune, devoted himself to landscape painting. Since landscape art was not highly regarded in his time, the elder Moreau was never received into the Academy and could not exhibit his work in the Salon until the 1790s, when access became unrestricted. In 1817, eleven years after his death, the genre was officially acknowledged, when a Prix de Rome in historical landscape was inaugurated. There is not much contemporary information about Moreau; it was not until the 1920s, with the publication of Georges Wildenstein's monograph and an exhibition of Moreau's work, that he received full recognition as a major eighteenth-century artist. More than a landscape painter, Moreau was clearly its most gifted practitioner in the difficult medium of gouache, which has the look of paint without its flexibility.

Moreau chose his paper carefully and achieved naturalistic, attractive results, as is evident in this large panoramic river view. Here the artist chose a very thin oriental paper, first preparing it with a layer of blue gouache and painting in the general outlines of the composition, simultaneously brushing most of the surface with a soft, broad brush to achieve atmospheric effects. Later he added color accents, notably in the little group of peasants with their herd of sheep and goats in the foreground.

Since Moreau apparently never left the Ile-de-France, most of his landscapes must have been based on views around Paris. Because of the difficulty of working in gouache, which dries quickly, there is little doubt that the bulk of his work was composed in the studio. The subject of this large, airy gouache is decidedly Italianate and suggests an awareness of the work of Marco Ricci, the Venetian landscape artist, who also worked in the medium. Moreau's silvery tones and naturalism anticipate the landscapes of Corot and other nineteenth-century Barbizon painters. CDD

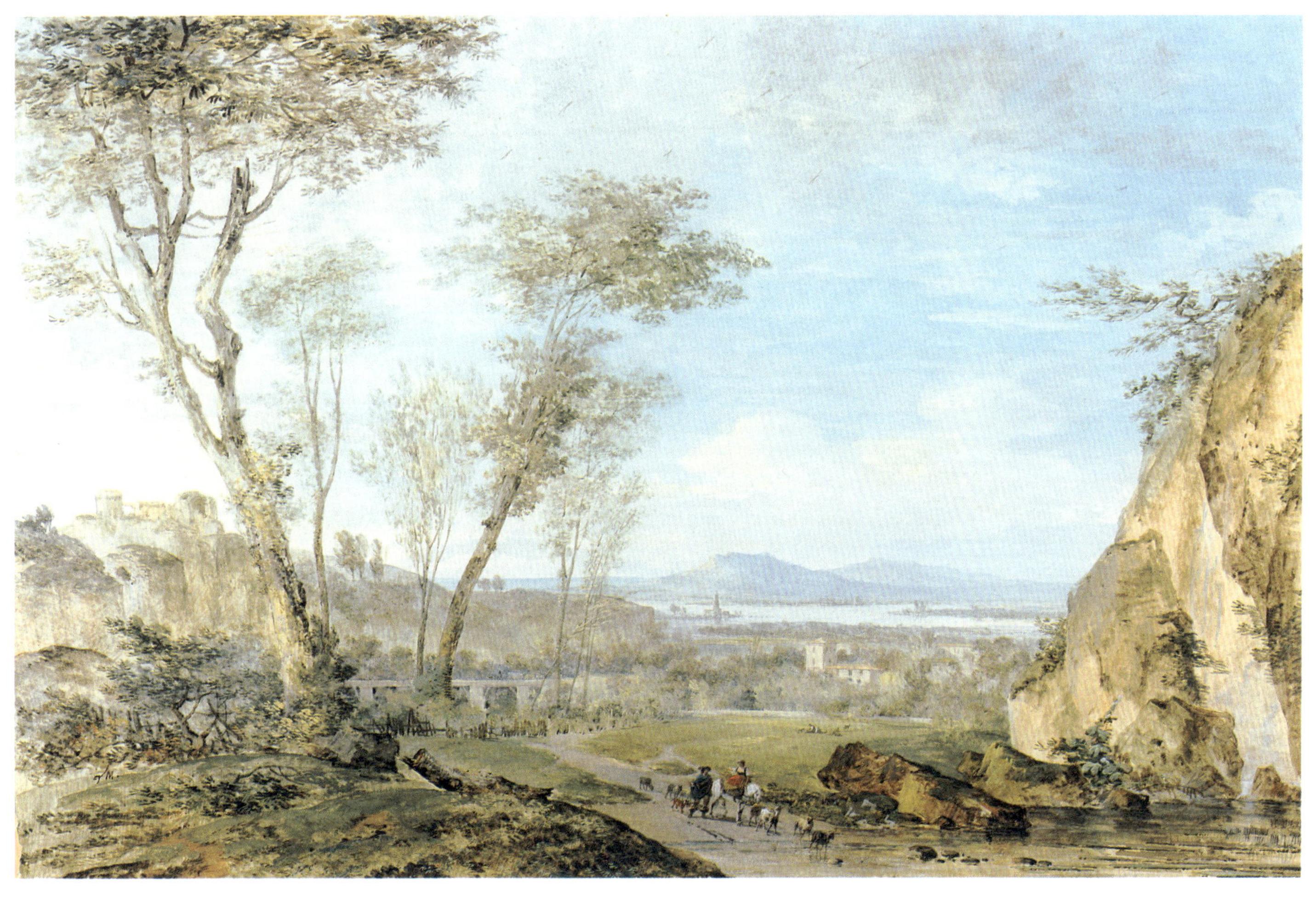

19

JEAN-BAPTISTE HUET

Paris 1745–1811 Paris

Studies of Corn Husks and Wheat

Watercolor and some gouache over black chalk. 10 x 15 1/2 inches (254 x 401 mm). Watermark: fragment with a letter *T* on a globe (cf. Heawood 2394). Signed and dated at lower left in pen and brown ink, *J.B. hüet 1792*; numbered in a different ink at upper left, *14*.

PROVENANCE: Kate de Rothschild, London.

BIBLIOGRAPHY: Rome 1991, under no. 85, p. 178 n. 2.

EXHIBITIONS: London 1990a, no. 38, repr.; Paris and New York 1993–94, no. 85, repr. (in color).

1992.2

Hüet is best known for his pastoral subjects, reminiscent of those of his mentors, Boucher (with whom he may have studied privately) and Leprince. He is also known for his animal paintings, which resemble those of Oudry, whom he admired. In this atypical work, however, Hüet has taken as his subject some very common plants. A few similar drawings have survived, notably the studies of a pumpkin, signed and dated 1785 and now in the Ashmolean Museum, Oxford (fig. 1; repr. Rome 1991, no. 85).

It is not known for what purpose Hüet drew these or why he very plausibly (as is indicated by the numbering) put them together sequentially in an album or portfolio. Although he often made highly finished botanical studies, these distinctive drawings are quite different in character and demonstrate a new sensibility, creating a modern still life unique in the art of the period. CDD

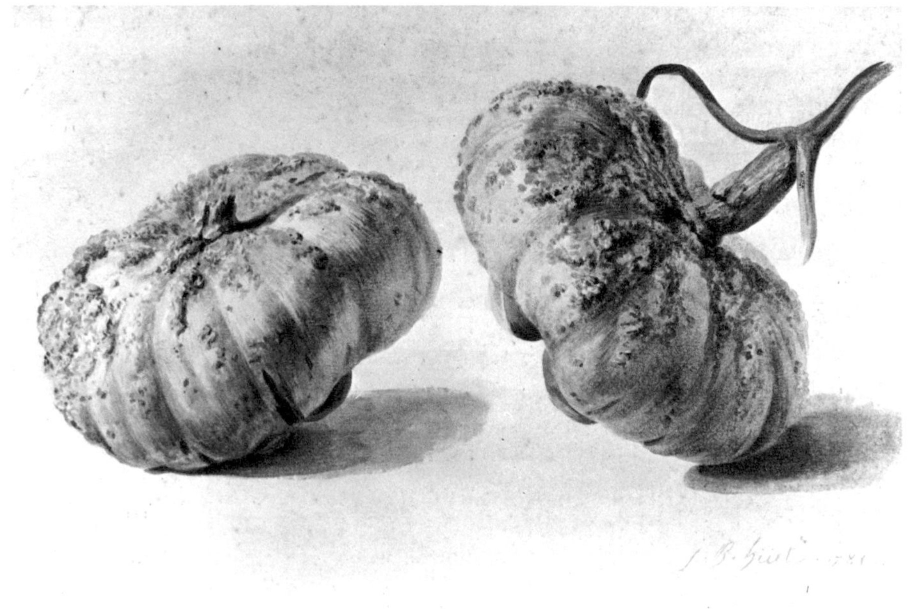

Fig. 1 Jean-Baptiste Hüet, *Two Studies of a Pumpkin*, Ashmolean Museum of Art and Archaeology, Oxford.

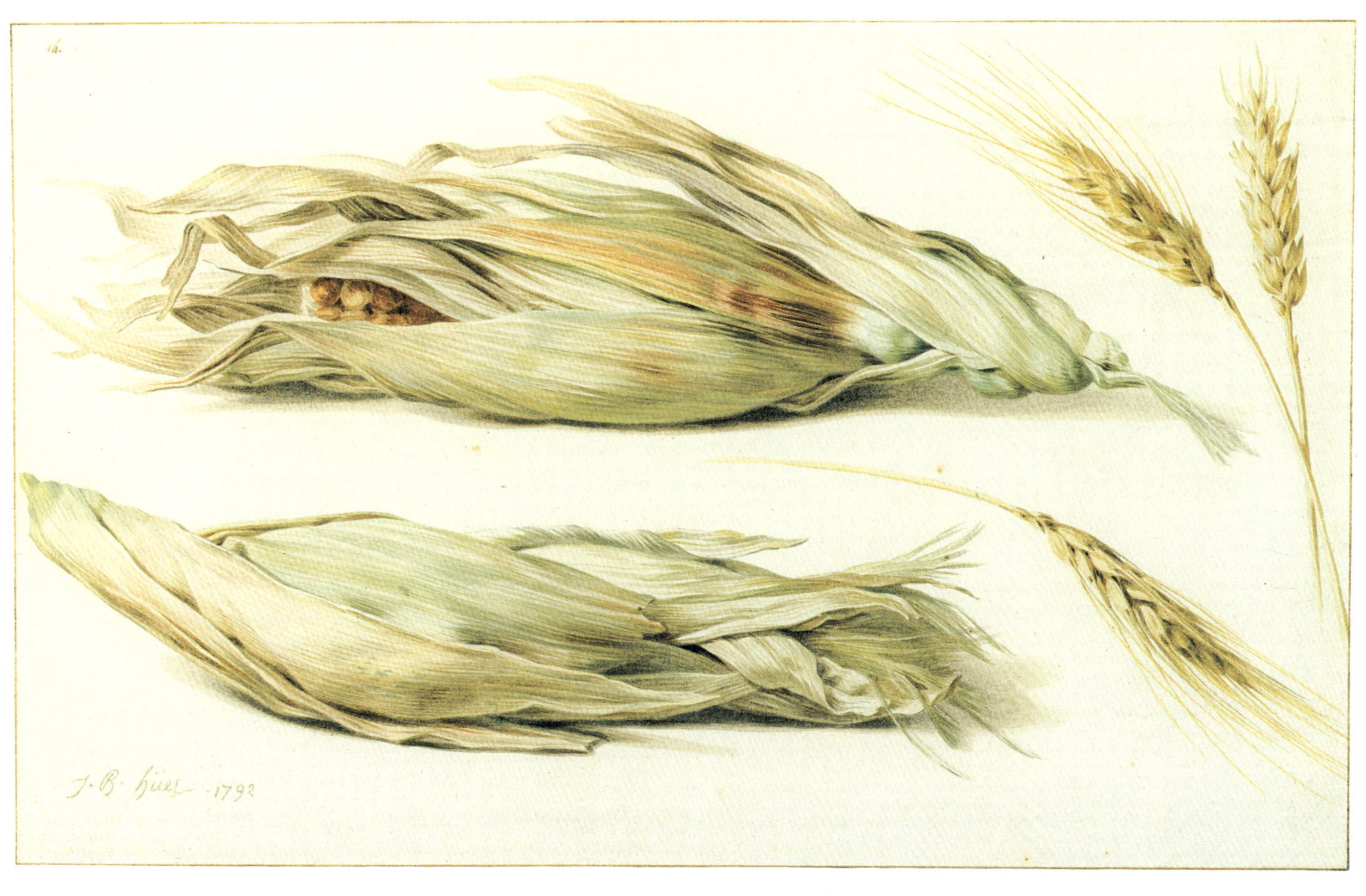

20

LOUIS-ROLAND TRINQUESSE

Paris ca. 1745–ca. 1800 Paris

Study of a Lady of Fashion

Red chalk. 14 13/16 x 10 1/16 inches (376 x 254 mm). Watermark: fragment of countermark with letters RH.

PROVENANCE: Edmond and Jules de Goncourt (Lugt 1089); their sale, Hôtel Drouot, Paris, 15–17 February 1897, lot 323; G. Menier, sale; Mlle Demarsy, lot 256; her sale; Comte Pierre de Jumilhac and others, sale, Paris, Galerie Georges Petit, 15 June 1929, no. 5, repr.; Richard Owen, Paris; John Nicholas Brown, Providence; David Tunick, New York; Thos. Agnew & Sons, Ltd., London.

BIBLIOGRAPHY: Agnew's 1992, p. 136, pl. 126, repr. (in color).

EXHIBITIONS: Paris 1929, no. 5, repr.; Providence 1931; Paris 1933a, no. 277; Omaha 1941; London 1989, no. 24, repr. (in color); Paris and New York 1993–94, no. 86, repr.

1990.16

Trinquesse, probably of Burgundian origin, was active in Paris from 1771 to 1797 (according to the dates on his drawings). This "crayonneur à la sanguine," as Edmond de Goncourt called him (Goncourt 1881, p. 164), specialized in studies of women in fashionable costumes posed in domestic surroundings. In this drawing, a young woman sits precariously on the edge of a narrow rectangular table, her head turned toward the spectator, supporting herself in this unstable position with her left hand. Originating from the Goncourt collection, it may be one of a series of twenty-four studies that, according to the artist, were made in 1773 after Madame de Franmery. Several drawings from this group were formerly in the Cailleux collection (Jean Cailleux, "The Drawings of Louis Roland Trinquesse," *Burlington Magazine* 116 [February 1974], ii–iv). One was sold in Paris on 28 March 1990 and is inscribed *17 février 1778*. The artist himself may have been mistaken about the 1773 date. Since the model in the latter study wears the same dress—known as a caraco gown because of its hip-length jacket, or caraco—the inscribed date must be right.

Trinquesse seems to have had three different models for these drawings. One was Marianne Franmery; the others, also identified on the basis of inscriptions, were Louise Charlotte Marini and Louise-Elizabeth Bain. The artist, however, was not interested in the facial expression or the individual attributes of his sitters; his preoccupation was the rendering of costume in every elegant detail (the flounced skirts and bodices as well as the fancy bonnets and plumed hats), which makes these drawings, fluently executed in the red chalk medium, small masterpieces in the genre of costume design. RSK

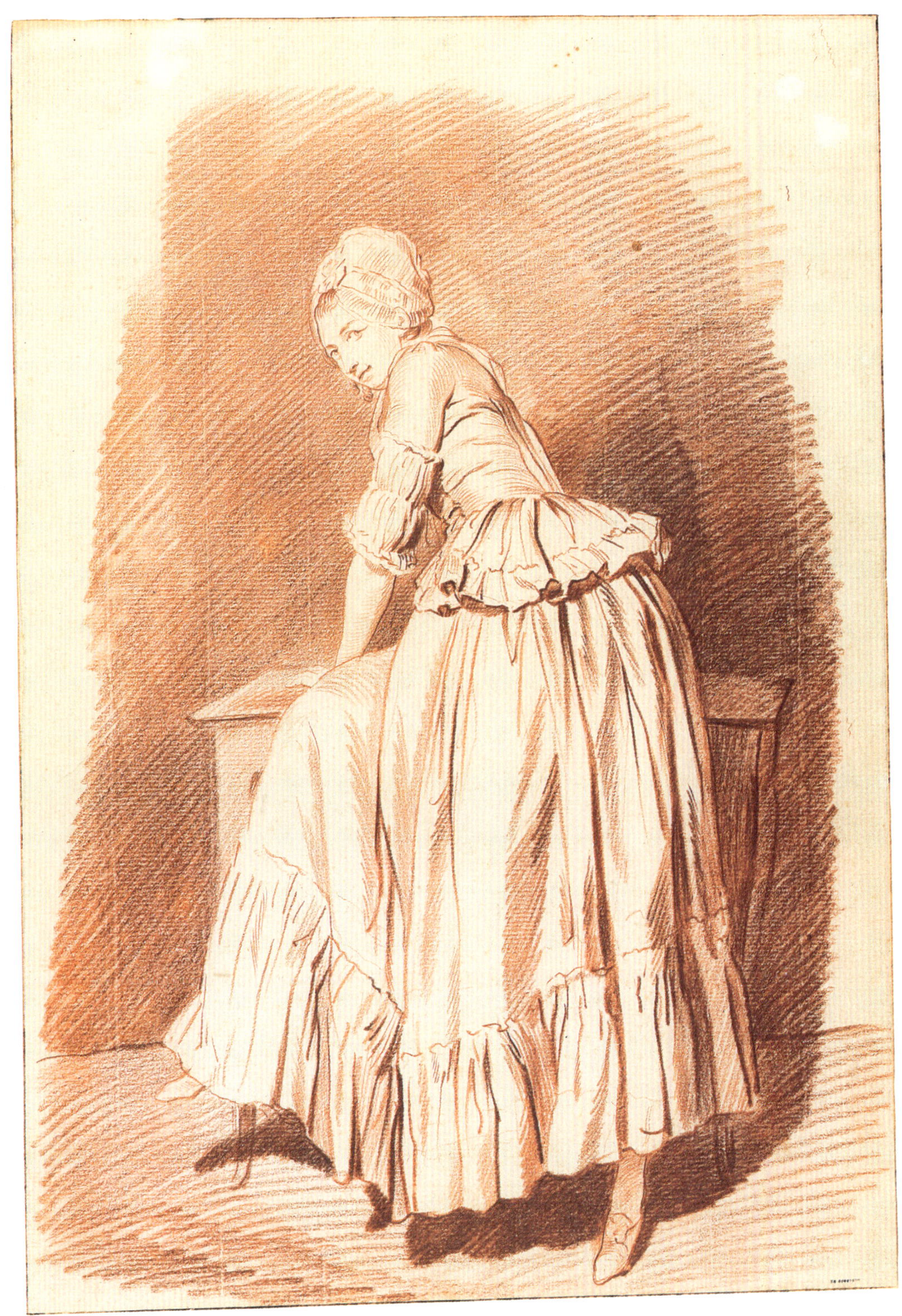

21

JACQUES-LOUIS DAVID

Paris 1748–1825 Brussels

An Alpine Landscape with a Horse-drawn Carriage

From album 10, one of David's *albums factices*, now dismembered. Black chalk, with traces of white. 6 x 8 3/8 inches (154 x 212 mm). Watermark: none.

PROVENANCE: Eugène and Jules David (Lugt 839 and Lugt 1437); A. Chassagnolle, 1835; private collection, New York; Bob P. Haboldt & Co., New York.

BIBLIOGRAPHY: Paris and Versailles 1989–90, p. 71, fig. 38; Montreal 1993, under no. 128.

EXHIBITION: Paris and New York 1991, no. 6, repr.

1991.6

This drawing is one of a group of eleven landscapes in album 10 of David's *albums factices*, which also contains a number of works after antiquities. There were originally twelve of these *albums factices*. Two of them, albums 7 and 9, went immediately to the Louvre at the time of the David sale in 1835, while the heirs and people closest to David obtained the remaining ten. Album 1 eventually went to the Fogg Art Museum as the bequest of Grenville L. Winthrop. Both albums 3 and 10 were on the New York art market in the 1950s. Album 3 was sold more or less intact to the Nationalmuseum, Stockholm, in 1959, but album 10 was dismembered and the leaves sold separately. Most recently album 11 was sold by a private collector and acquired by the J. Paul Getty Center for the History of Art and the Humanities, Santa Monica.

David visited Switzerland in July and August of 1815 and made a number of drawings around Lake Leman and Chamonix. An unfinished sketchbook made during this trip, which now belongs to a private collector in Paris, was published in 1969 (Sérullaz 1969, pp. 65–68). There are drawings on only thirteen of the seventy-four leaves in this sketchbook, six of which are landscapes. These landscapes are somewhat smaller than this one and are drawn on blue paper; however, they were similarly executed in black chalk or graphite. There is very little correspondence of the views, although they seem to have been executed in a similarly mountainous area. It is entirely plausible that the von Bülow example was executed at the same time in a different sketchbook from which eventually it was removed and mounted in album 10.

In addition to this drawing, the Library has acquired drawings of the Campidoglio and Castel Sant'Angelo; all three of these landscapes were on folio 17 of the album before it was dismembered (Montreal 1993, no. 128, repr.).

A thematic study of the albums reveals that single figures appeared first, masculine before feminine (which were more numerous). These were followed by studies after compositions (paintings and antique groups), landscapes, isolated elements (such as heads and furniture), and finally the calques. From this reconstruction, it was determined that forty-six pages were reserved for landscapes (Sérullaz 1969, p. 18 n. 10).

CDD

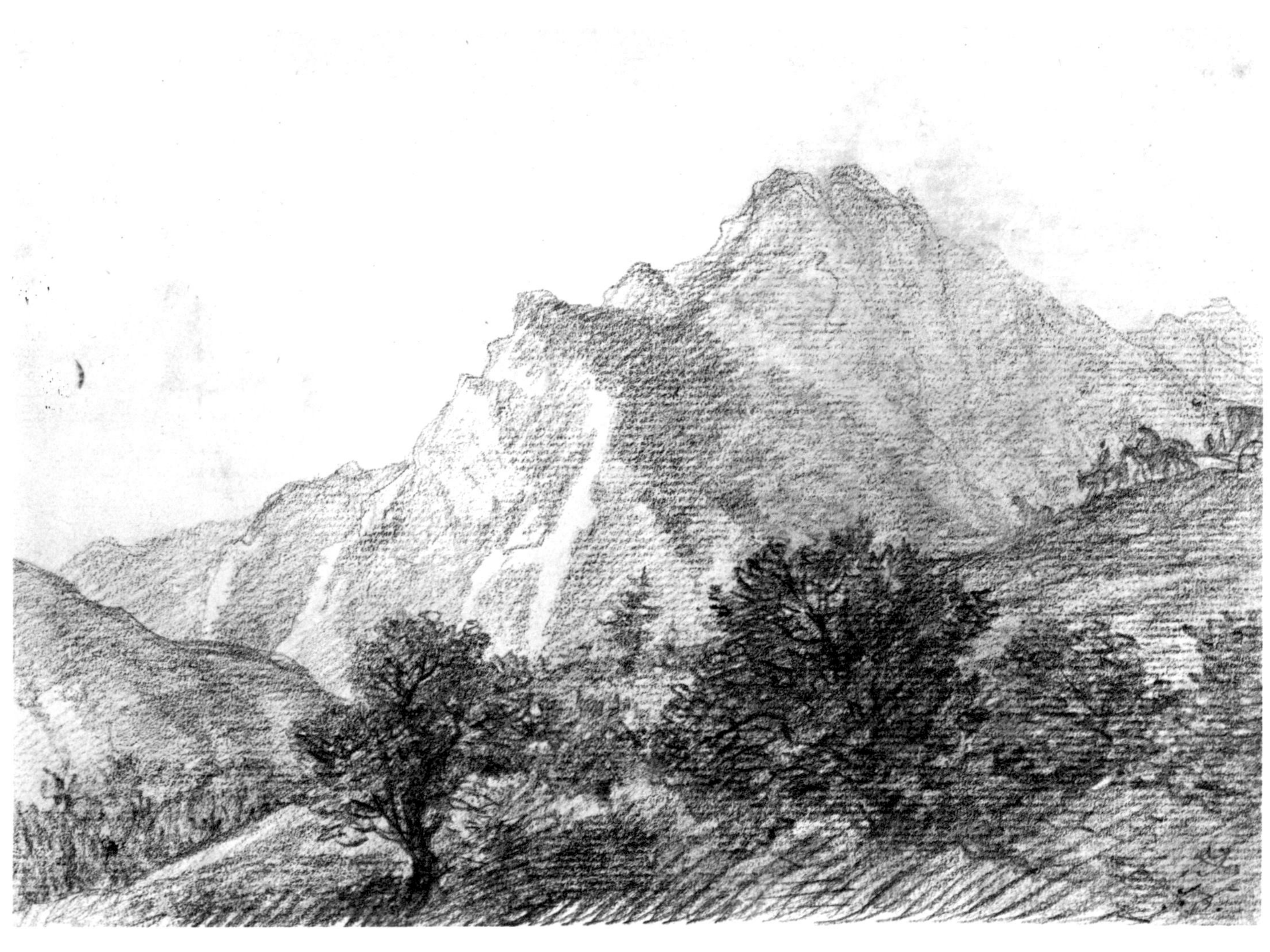

22

CLAUDE-LOUIS CHATELET

Paris 1753–1794 Paris

View of the Island of Capri

Watercolor over preliminary drawing in black chalk. 9 1/16 x 13 11/16 inches (231 x 347 mm). Watermark: fleur-de-lis and D. & C. Blauw [cut off]. Divided into quadrants in pencil on verso, which is inscribed variously, in pen and dark brown ink, *J R, no. 66; 72.23*, and, in a different brown ink, *no. 1 p*, and at top of page, *139*. Also inscribed in pencil at lower left of old mount (onto which some of the inscriptions on the verso of the drawing have offset), *Vue de l'ile de Capri prise de la maison de Tibere / Engraved in St. Non. Voyage Pictoresque* [sic] *des Naples et Sicile*.

PROVENANCE: possibly James Reiss (Lugt 1522); possibly sale, Paris, Hôtel Drouot, 4 November 1970, no. 45, repr.; sale, New York, Sotheby's, 12 January 1994, lot 167, repr. (in color).

1994.2

While this drawing was undoubtedly made in connection with the *Voyage pittoresque des Naples et Sicile*, the composition does not actually appear in the abbé de Saint-Non's travel book. This ambitious project was in preparation for over two decades, and, by the late 1770s, the abbé had entrusted the work of obtaining more illustrations to Baron Vivant-Denon, who was attached to the French embassy in Naples at the time. It was Vivant-Denon who recruited Desprez and Chatelet for the project. Around 1778 Chatelet, along with Hoüel, Desprez, and P. A. Pâris, went to Naples, where each executed a number of views. Located in the third of four volumes, the section on Capri is illustrated by two entirely different views, both evidently based on views of the island from the sea, including one of its harbor (figs. 1 and 2). Vivant-Denon and his party arrived at Capri after a boat journey from Naples prolonged to four and a half hours by ill winds and other factors. They stayed overnight in a sailor's house that afforded an excellent view of the island of Ischia and of Naples, Vesuvius, and the coast of Sorrento, explored the entire island, and no doubt made many on-site drawings.

This watercolor was sufficiently attractive for Chatelet to copy exactly at least once, for there is another rendering of it now on the art market in Paris (sale, London, Sotheby's, 4 July 1994, lot 135, repr.). Since the island is composed of dramatic limestone outcroppings, it is difficult to say with certainty what the view represents. It might be the rocks at Lo Capo on the northeast corner of the island, where the villa of Tiberius is located. It is also possible that we are looking at a less dramatic and foreshortened view of the main marina taken from the left side of the saddle-shaped harbor. This seems less likely, however, if the inscription on the mount has any basis in fact, for the main marina is on the north side of the island, far from Tiberius's villa. Chatelet's composition includes the usual gesticulating figures who point excitedly at the spectacular rock formations. Figures such as these are often employed for staffage and scale as well as dramatic emphasis.

Chatelet executed many views for the *Voyage pittoresque* as well as other travel publications, including the abbé de La Borde's *Tableaux topographiques, pittoresques, physiques, historiques, moraux, politiques, littéraires de la Suisse* (3 vols., Paris, 1780–86). In 1989, the Library acquired its first Chatelet drawing (1989.43), which most likely was intended for the Swiss series. In this work, the artist employed the quite different technique of ink and wash, heightened with white on blue paper.

CDD

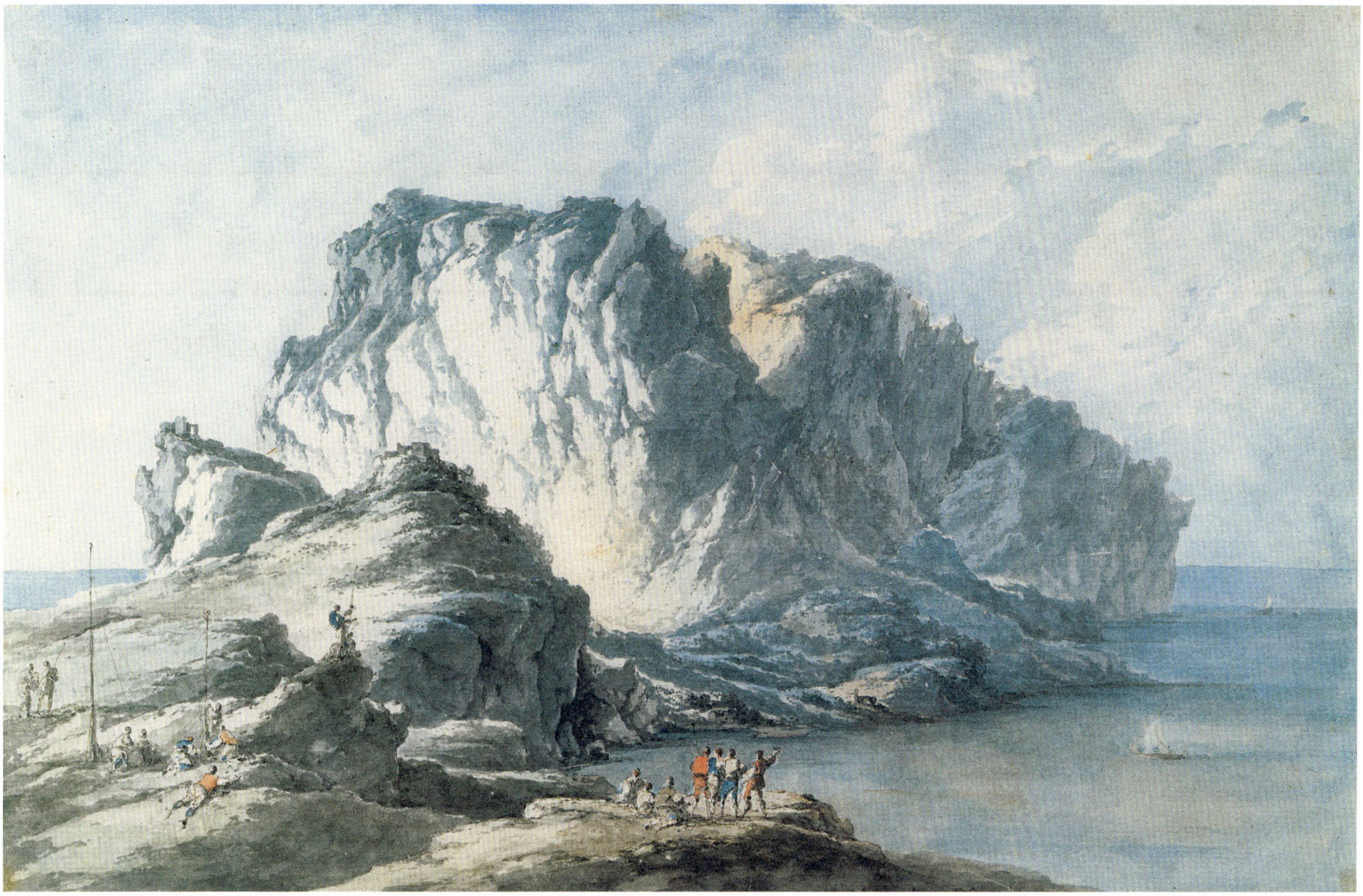

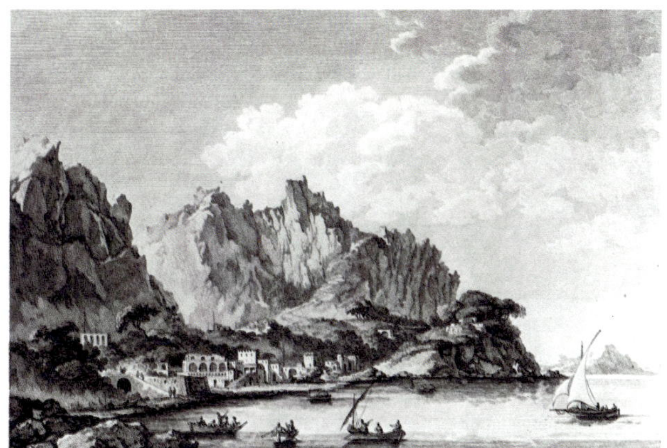

Fig. 1 Claude-Louis Chatelet, *View of the Island of Capri*, in *Voyage pittoresque des Naples et Sicile* (vol. III, pl. 97), The Pierpont Morgan Library, PML 62643++.

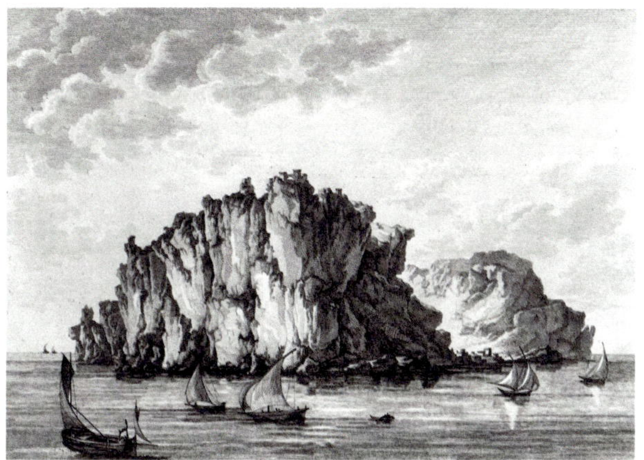

Fig. 2 Claude-Louis Chatelet, *View of the Island of Capri*, in *Voyage pittoresque des Naples et Sicile* (vol. III, pl. 98), The Pierpont Morgan Library, PML 62643++.

23

VICTOR-JEAN NICOLLE

Paris 1754–1826 Paris

The Temple of Vesta, Rome

Watercolor, pen and brown ink, over preliminary indications in black chalk; ruled border in pen and brown ink. 8 1/16 x 12 1/4 inches (205 x 309 mm). Watermark: none visible through lining. Signed at middle left, in pen and brown ink, *V. J. Nicolle*; inscribed on back of old mount, by the artist, *Vue du Temple de Vesta, Situé au bord du tibre; prise du Coté de Transtevere* [sic]; *à Rome*.

PROVENANCE: Jean Baptiste de Meryan, marquis de Lagoy (Lugt 1710); Raymond Ferrier (Lugt S. 2207a); his sale, Paris, E. Pape, 24 December 1924 (with its pendant drawing, *Le Temple de la Concorde, Rome*); private collection, southern France; Galerie Cailleux, Paris.

BIBLIOGRAPHY: PML/*FR* XX, 1984, pp. 282–83.

EXHIBITIONS: New York PML 1984, no. 88; New York PML 1989; Montreal 1993, no. 111, repr.

1983.32

Born in Paris, Nicolle was a student at Bachelier's school and worked under the architect Petit-Radel. Spending a good deal of his time in Rome, where he seems to have first traveled in 1779, again between 1787 and 1799, and once more from 1806 to 1810, he became one of the most attractive recorders of the Italian scene. Since Nicolle signed but did not date this large watercolor, it is not known precisely when it or its pendant, *The Temple of Concord*, was executed (fig. 1). Both were originally in the collection of the marquis de Lagoy (1764–1829), the well-known collector who owned more than three thousand drawings and was deputy for Aix-en-Provence under the restoration. The pair stayed together until 1983; *The Temple of Concord* was purchased for the Phillips Family Collection in 1984 (repr. Montreal 1993, no. 112). These drawings are quite similar in size to another pair of highly finished Roman views in the Louvre, *Le Ponte Rotto à Rome* [sic] (204 x 312 mm; R.F. 14628) and *La Place Trajane à Rome, avec la Colonne et l'Eglise de Sainte Marie de Lorette à Rome* (202 x 310 mm; R.F. 14629). CDD

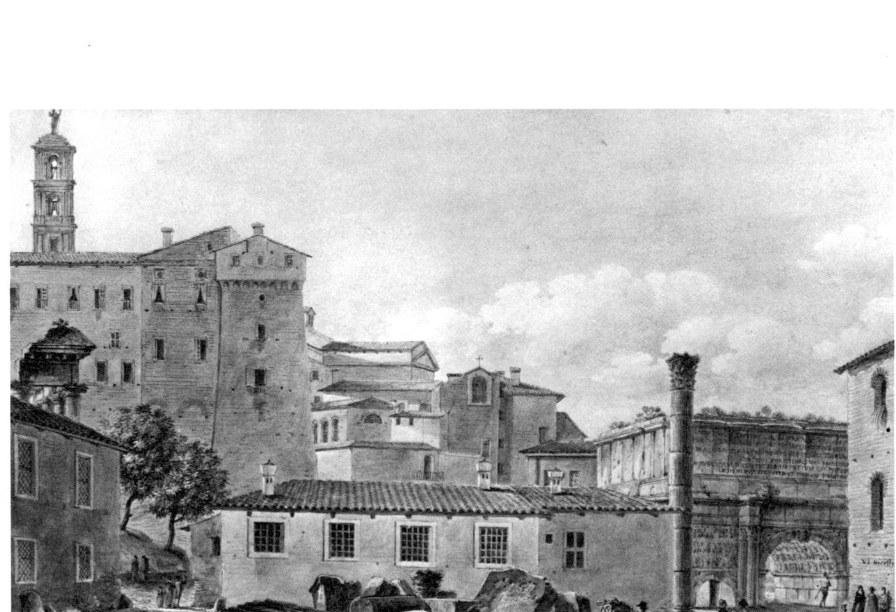

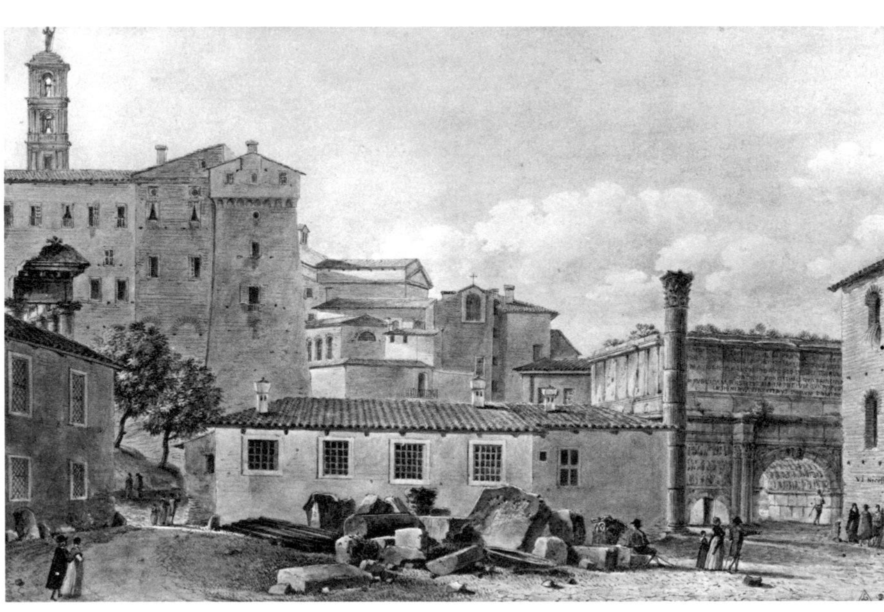

Fig. 1 Victor-Jean Nicolle, *The Temple of Concord*, the Phillips Family Collection.

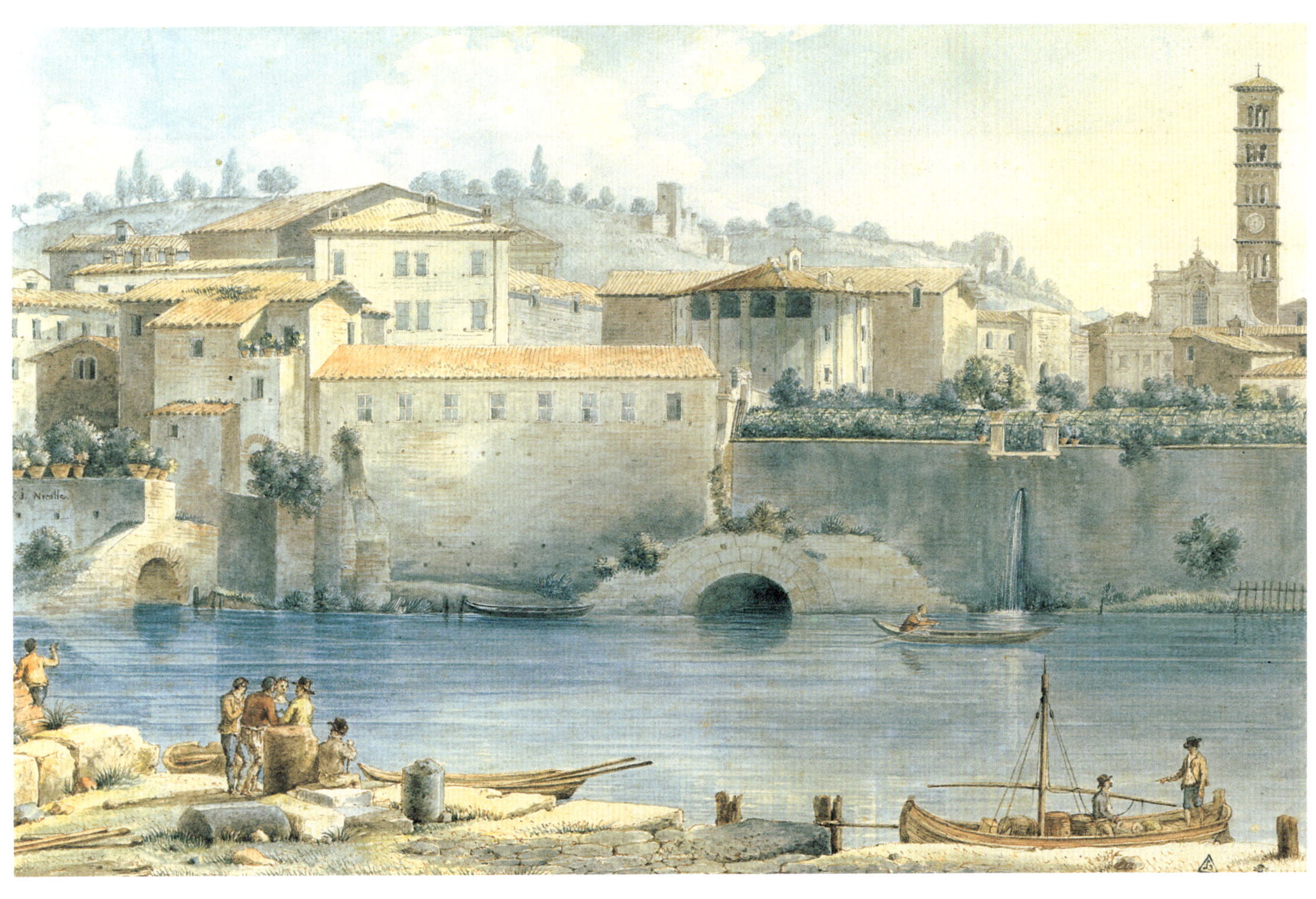

24

JEAN-BAPTISTE MALLET

Grasse 1759–1835 Paris

Domestic Interior Including a Seated Young Woman Feeding a Child

Gouache. 7 7/8 x 10 7/16 inches (200 x 265 mm). Watermark: none visible through lining. Inscribed in pen and brown ink in an eighteenth-century hand on old framing paper, *Mallet.*

PROVENANCE: probably sale, Paris, Hôtel Drouot, 20 October 1975, lot 75, not repr.; probably sale, Paris, Hôtel Drouot, 7 May 1976, lot 46, not repr.; Rosenberg & Stiebel, New York.

1990.25

At first sight this scene of domesticity is reminiscent of Greuze, but there is no moral or subtext here. "Peintre de genre, peintre de mœurs," Mallet is best known and admired as an illustrator of late eighteenth- and early nineteenth-century life. The artist, the prolific *petit-maître* of the Empire genre, is in a sense the heir to the Baudouin or Lavreince tradition.

The tranquil scene depicted here with such graceful intimacy is evidently set during winter. A mother brings a bowl of steaming food to a small boy who reaches for it; another rather contemplative young woman stands at the table, her left arm resting on a basket. At the left, a young man warms himself in front of the fire, as does an elderly seated woman with her back to the viewer. Throughout the room a few details add interest to the otherwise sparse furnishings: A curtain, which probably serves as a room divider, is flung aside; a small still life of glassware and crockery occupies a shelf at the right. Some chickens forage for crumbs of bread or grain, while a hungry cat stares at the bowl of hot food.

Mallet studied with Prud'hon as well as Merimée. He first showed at the Academy in 1791 and received a second-place medal; he would have to wait until 1817 for his first. One contemporary critic, Jansen, wrote in highly complimentary terms of the finesse of Mallet's touch and color sense: "on ne peut traiter la gouache avec une touche plus fraîche et plus spirituelle." While the artist's technique in watercolor and gouache is remarkable, much of the charm or appeal of his work for the late twentieth-century viewer is due to his curiously mannered subject matter. CDD

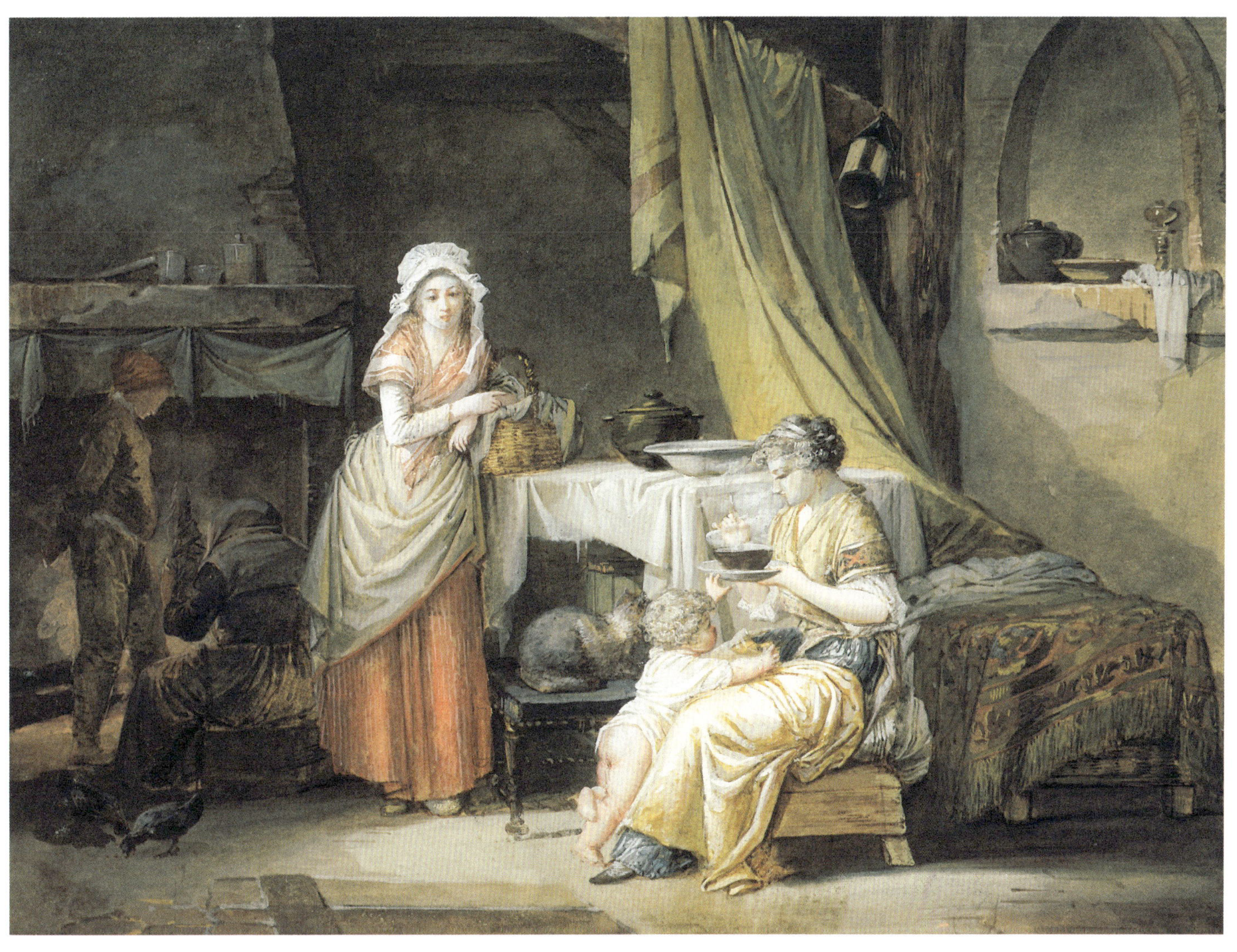

25

GUILLAUME GUILLON, called LETHIERE

Sainte-Anne, Guadeloupe 1760–1832 Paris

Classical Subject, Possibly Electra at the Tomb of Agamemnon

Point of brush and black and brown ink, brown and gray wash, some green chalk and white gouache, over black chalk and some graphite, on wove paper. 18 5/16 x 23 1/2 inches (466 x 597 mm). Watermark: none. Signed, inscribed, and dated by the artist, in pen and brown ink on base of tomb at right, *G.. Le thiere a paris 1796.*

PROVENANCE: Elisabeth Royer, Paris.

1994.7

Lethière, a student of Doyen, took only second place in the competition for the Rome prize but was awarded the status of a *pensionnaire* at the French Academy in Rome in 1786. Returning to Paris four years later, he opened an atelier, proving to be a popular teacher and exhibiting regularly at the Salons from 1793 until 1831. In 1804, he accompanied Lucien Bonaparte to Spain, where he organized an exhibition of Spanish masters. Replacing Joseph Suvée (1743–1807), Lethière was named director of the French Academy in Rome in 1807, serving in this capacity until 1819. Ingres was a *pensionnaire* during his term at the French Academy, and Lethière was the subject of his drawings, most notably the portrait of him in the Library's collection (1977.56). Returning to Paris, Lethière became a professor at the Ecole des Beaux-Arts and resumed private teaching. He transferred his studio to the Institut de France in 1822. A neoclassical artist, he nearly always drew inspiration from Greek and Roman history and drama. While in Rome in 1788, Lethière, like David, treated the subject of Brutus condemning his sons to death. This oil sketch, which he sent from Rome in 1788 and was eventually exhibited in the Salon of 1795 and again in 1801, is now known only through a highly finished drawing in the Musée Municipal, Château-Gontier.

Geneviève Capy, who is preparing a monograph on the artist, has suggested that the subject of this large, finely worked drawing is Electra led to the tomb of her father, Agamemnon. Electra did not attend her father's funeral but secretly visited his tomb. There she saw her brother Orestes again, newly returned to Argos and sworn to avenge their father's death. He revealed his plan to Electra, who vowed to help him. The male figures depicted at the right of the tomb are obviously Orestes and Pylades.

Both Aeschylus and Euripides told the horrifying story of Agamemnon's murder and the reaction of his children (Orestes, Electra, Iphigenia, and Chrisothemis). On his return from the Trojan Wars, Agamemnon was murdered by his wife, Clytemnestra, and her lover, Aegisthus. Timeless in its appeal, the intriguing story had a particular currency during the late eighteenth and early nineteenth centuries. At least six original plays, including one by Voltaire, and an equal number of operas based on the Orestes story were performed during the eighteenth century in Paris alone. The English artist Flaxman also depicted Electra at the tomb in a friezelike composition, with a procession of mourning women carrying gifts to the deceased.

Examples of Lethière's draughtsmanship were included in *Visions of Antiquity,* shown at the Los Angeles County Museum of Art, the Philadelphia Museum of Art, and the Minneapolis Institute of Arts, 1993–94, nos. 51, 52, repr. CDD

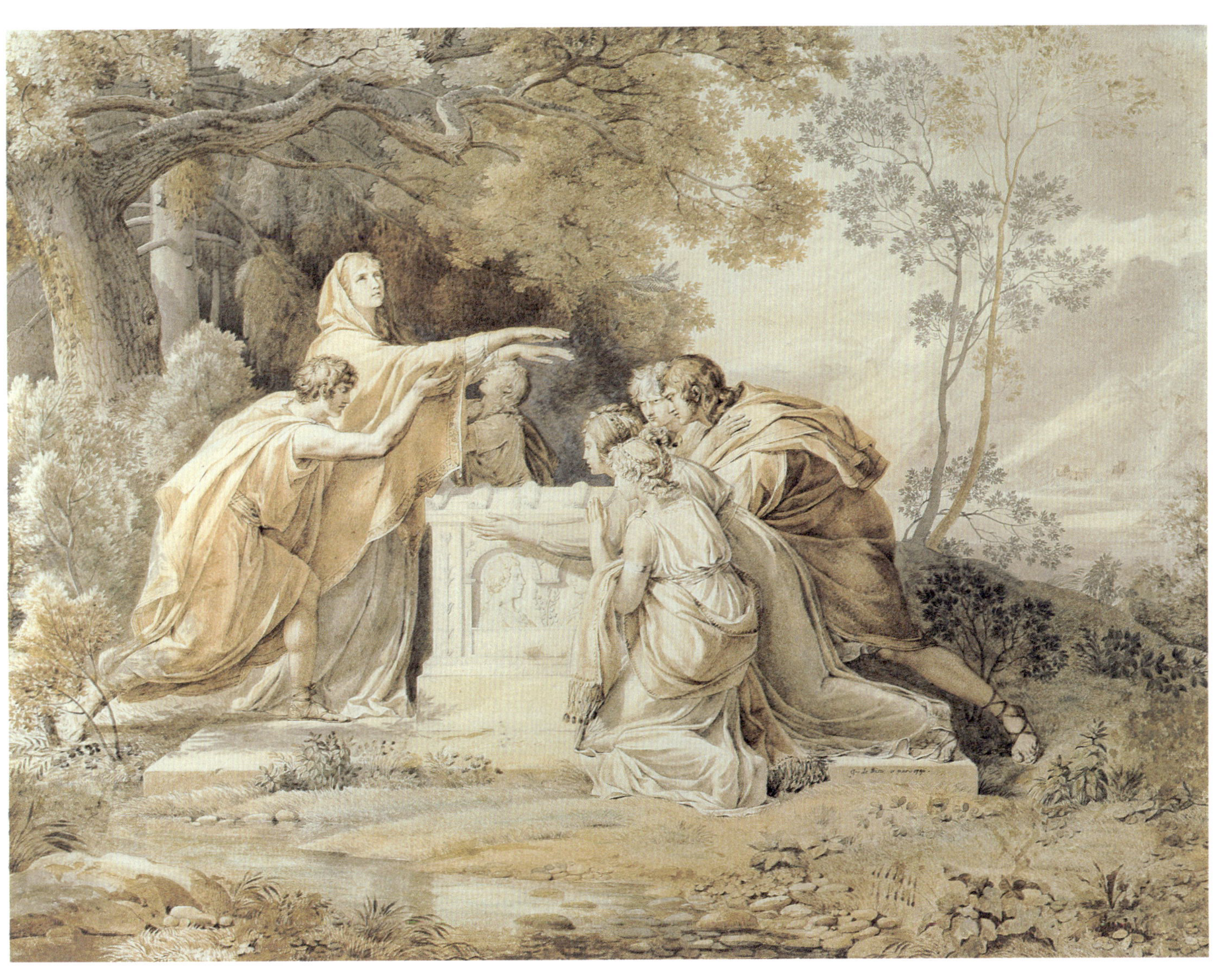

26

LOUIS LEOPOLD BOILLY

La Bassée 1761–1845 Paris

Standing Man Seen Three-Quarter Length, Facing Left

Black chalk, heightened with white, on brown wove paper. 10 1/2 x 9 7/8 inches (268 x 239 mm).

PROVENANCE: unidentified collector's dry stamp FM; sale, London, Christie's, 8 December 1976, lot 113, pl. 43 (as *Study of a Tailor*).

BIBLIOGRAPHY: Russell 1977, p. 153, fig. 116; PML/*FR* XVIII, 1978, p. 249; Siegfried 1990, p. 520, pl. 61.

EXHIBITIONS: New York PML 1984, no. 95; Paris and New York 1993–94, no. 97, repr.

1977.38

This study is part of Boilly's elaborate preparations for *Les Déménagements*, the painting that Boilly exhibited in the Salon of 1822 and is now in the Art Institute of Chicago (fig. 1). The artist carefully constructed this genre subject to depict the spectacle of ordinary people moving their belongings through the streets to find new lodgings. Although Boilly's model in this drawing was middle-aged, in the painting the artist ultimately transformed him into the older, bald man who is seen at the right of the composition, loading boxes onto a barrow. In this study, Boilly examines the effect of the light on the textures of the man's costume, especially his shirt. The subject was successful, and a print after the composition was made by Jean-Henri Marlet (Siegfried 1990, pl. 63). A large watercolor sketch of the entire subject is now in the Musée des Beaux-Arts, Lille, and the Musée Cognacq-Jay, Paris, has an oil replica that the artist made in 1840. CDD

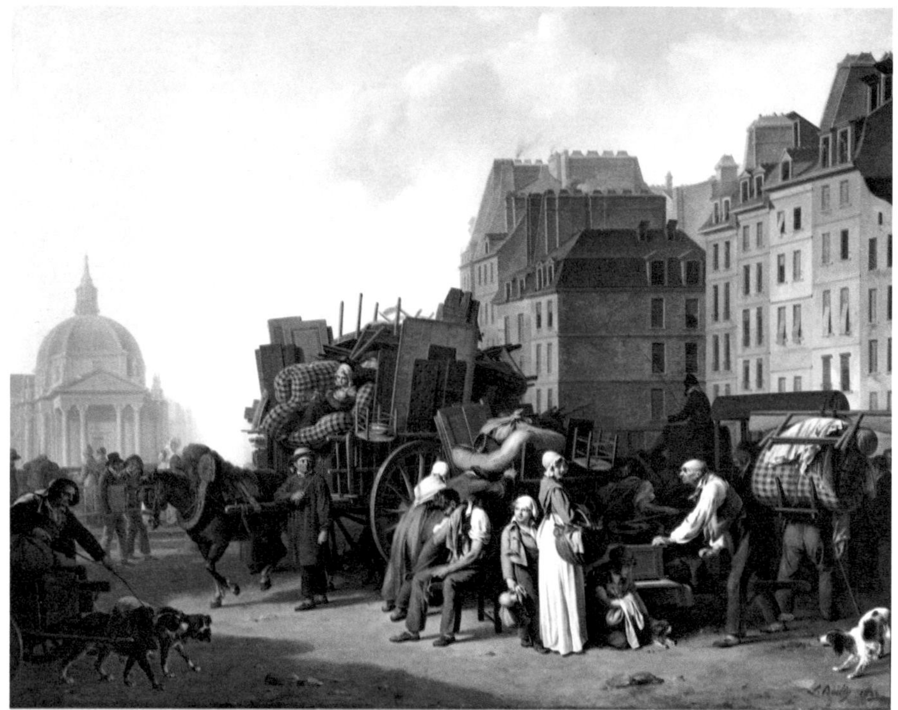

Fig. 1 Louis Léopold Boilly, *Les Déménagements sur le Port au Blé*, Art Institute of Chicago, 1982.494.

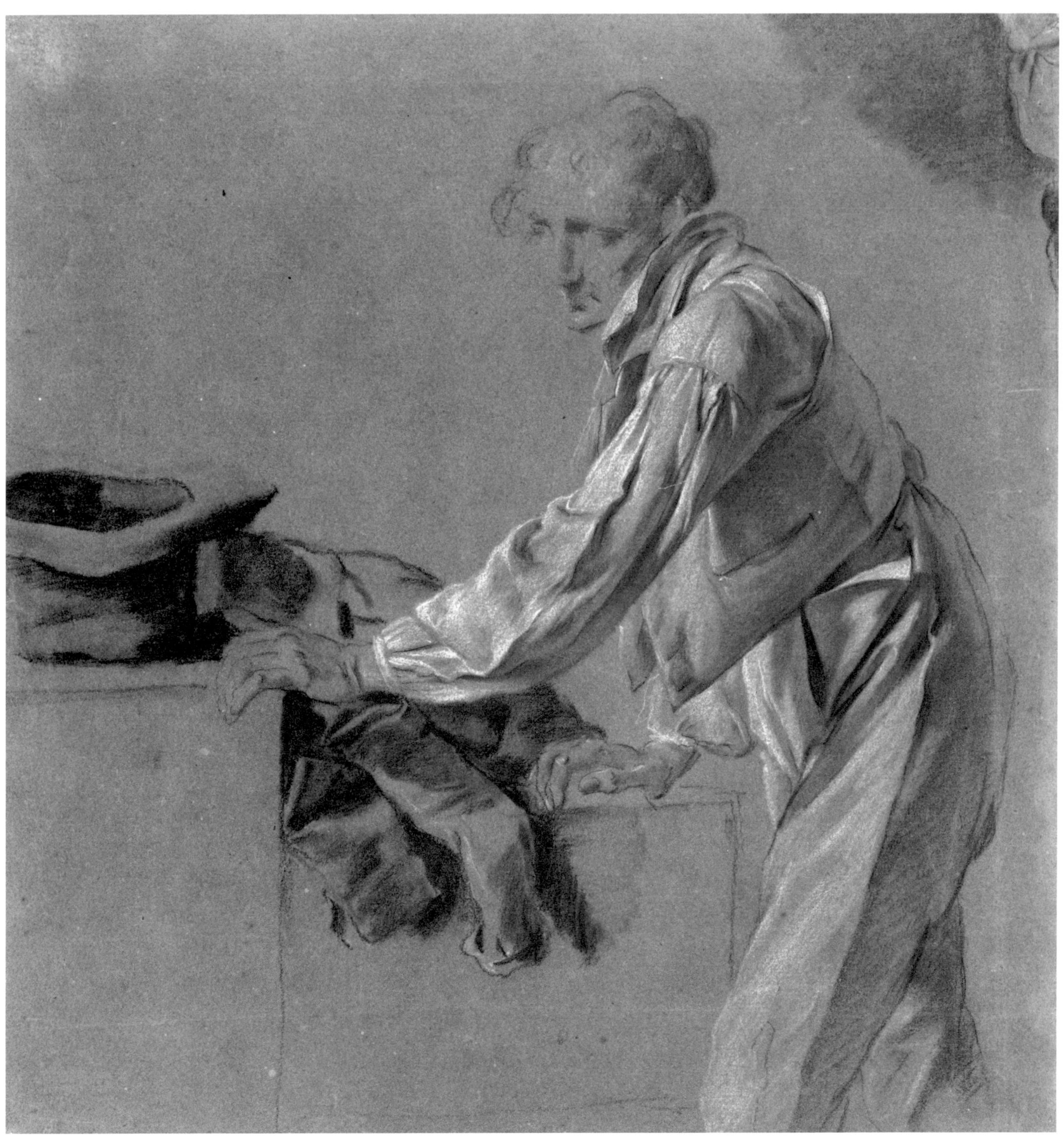

61

27

NICOLAS HUET, THE YOUNGER

Paris 1770–after 1828 Paris

Study of the Giraffe Given to Charles X by the Viceroy of Egypt, 1827

Watercolor and some gouache, over a few traces of black chalk. 10 1/16 x 7 5/8 inches (254 x 194 mm). Signed and dated, in pen and brown ink, at lower left, *huet 1827*; numbered for scale at lower right, *1/16*.

PROVENANCE: part of an album formed by a nineteenth-century collector, south of France; by descent; Bruno de Bayser, Paris; Galerie de Bayser, Paris; Kate de Rothschild and Didier Aaron, London and New York.

EXHIBITION: New York and elsewhere 1993, no. 52, repr. (in color).

1994.1

As a specialist in depicting animals and plants, Nicolas Hüet, the son of Jean-Baptiste Hüet (No. 19), was the official painter for the Musée d'Histoire Naturelle de la Ménagerie of the empress Joséphine. In 1827 he must have been one of the first to paint the much-celebrated giraffe, the "belle enfant des tropiques," as he was known, the first ever to be seen in France. The giraffe was presented to Charles X by the viceroy of Egypt. After a long and difficult journey from Egypt to Marseilles and then to Paris, which was followed by a large, formal reception at the Orangerie at Saint-Cloud, during the course of which Charles X held out a handful of rose petals to the animal in a ceremonial gesture of homage, the giraffe was properly settled into his new home in the Jardin des Plantes, Paris. He was seen by over 600,000 visitors in his first six months there alone. In 1845, he died at the age of twenty-one, having been the direct impetus for a girafferie craze that engendered, among other things, giraffe-patterned china services, rugs, and upholstered furniture. *Une Girafe pour le roi*, an exhibition devoted to him and the decorative objects he inspired, was held at the Musée de l'Ile-de-France, Château de Sceaux, in 1984.

Hüet's meticulously worked portrait shows the giraffe in his new home with one of the three pashas who came with him in attendance. Another portrait of the giraffe, also by Hüet, this time painted on vellum, has recently appeared on the art market (fig. 1). The pose of the animal is very similar in both examples, but the latter lacks a full landscape setting because it was executed in the official style of the Musée d'Histoire Naturelle. It includes an inscription in gold identifying the portrait as a present for the viceroy of Egypt, in gratitude for his gift. Whether it was ever sent is not known. CDD

Fig. 1 Nicolas Hüet, the Younger, *Portrait of a Giraffe*, Hazlitt, Gooden & Fox, London.

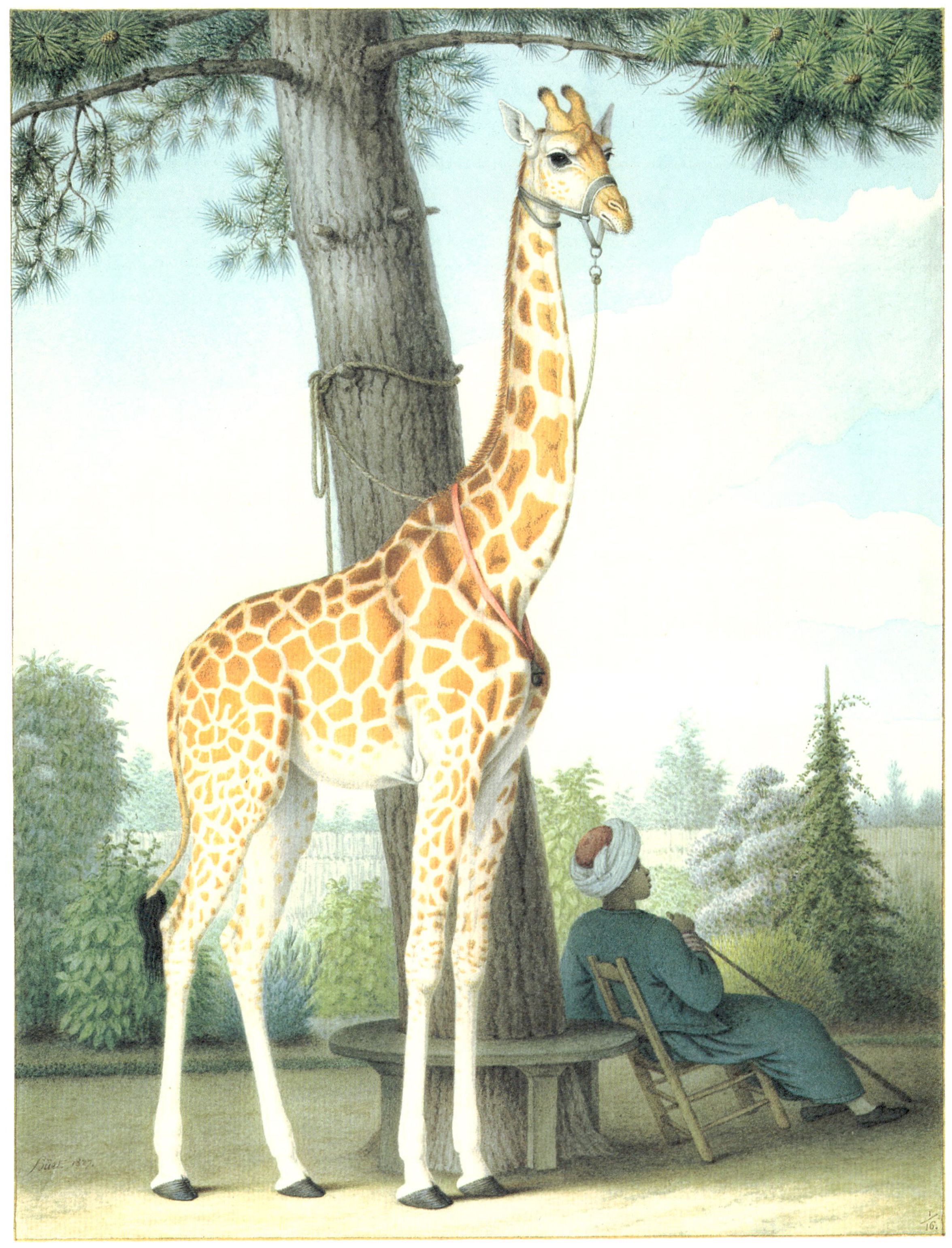

28

JEAN AUGUSTE DOMINIQUE INGRES

Montauban 1780–1867 Paris

Portrait of a Boy

Graphite, with touches of red watercolor in the hat and on the lapels of the boy's jacket; bordered by the artist in green watercolor. Full roundel sheet: 4 3/4 inches (106 mm). Diameter of design area: 3 5/16 inches (84 mm). Watermark: none. Signed (?) at lower right, in graphite, *Ingres*.

PROVENANCE: Saint-André family, Montauban; Mme Mathias-Edouard Pauvert; her daughter, Mme Abel Marche; her daughter, Mme Carrive; her son, Jean Carrive, Sainte-Foy-la-Grande; his wife, Mme Jean Carrive, Sainte-Foy-la-Grande; Mr. and Mrs. Germain Seligman, New York; E. V. Thaw & Co., Inc., New York.

BIBLIOGRAPHY: Naef 1970, p. 221ff., repr. p. 226; Sainte-Foy-la-Grande 1970, p. 11; Naef 1977–80, I, p. 38, no. 5, repr., IV, p. 16, no. 6; Richardson 1979, no. 34, repr.; MacGregor 1979, p. 740, repr.; PML/*FR* XX, 1984, pp. 265–66.

1982.2

This roundel profile drawing of an attractive young boy demonstrates Ingres's early interest in portraiture. He studied first with his father, who was an artist and sculptor as well as a musician. By 1793, the earliest possible date for this portrait, when Ingres would have been thirteen, he was already at work at the Toulouse Academy, studying with Joseph Roques, a friend of Jacques-Louis David. Although there would have been no opportunity for interaction between the two at this time, it must be noted that there is a certain stylistic affinity with David, who also drew a number of small roundel portraits. It may have been through Roques that Ingres became acquainted with this manner of portraiture, or perhaps both David and Ingres were emulating a common artistic example, such as Cochin or Augustin de Saint-Aubin, both of whom are well known for profile-portrait drawings and prints.

The boy, who wears a revolutionary bonnet and jacket resembling that worn by the Garde Nationale, was the nephew of André Jeanbon Saint-André, the Huguenot clergyman who supported the Jacobins and Robespierre during the French Revolution. Although it has been noted that Ingres's signature lacks the fluidity usually associated with an autograph, there is no doubt that the portrait is from Ingres's own hand. The signature may well be an inscription that was added later. Both the artist's and subject's families lived in Montauban, and this portrait remained in the Saint-André family until 1972. CDD

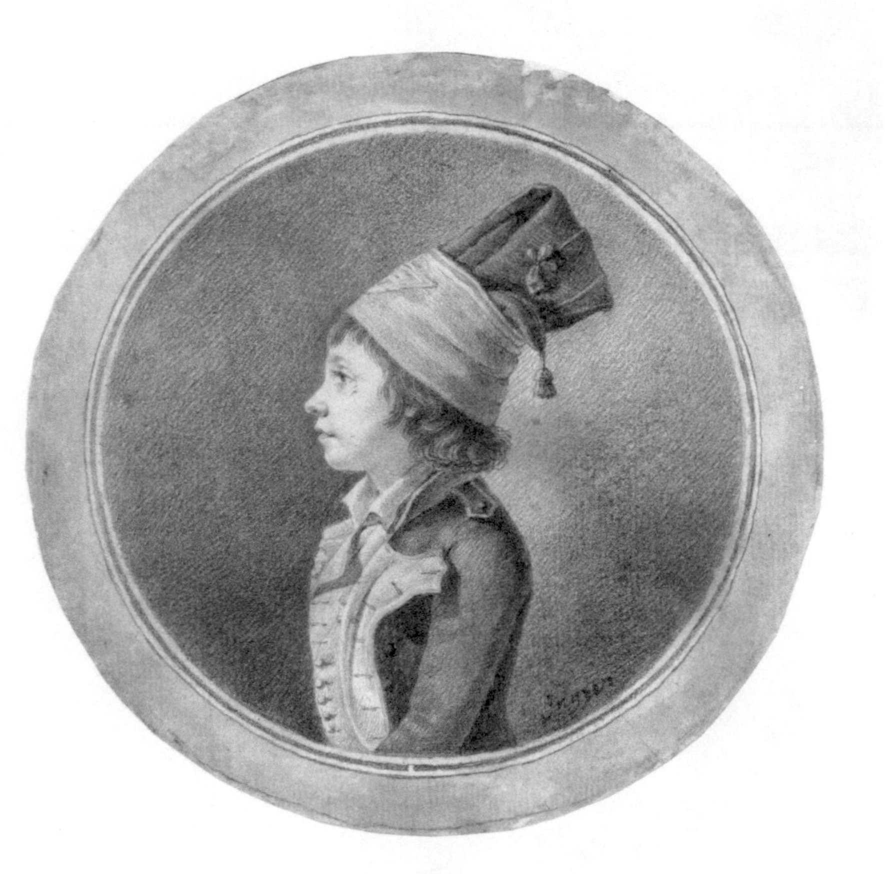

29

JEAN AUGUSTE DOMINIQUE INGRES

Montauban 1780–1867 Paris

Portrait of Charles Désiré Norry (1796–1818)

Pencil on wove paper. 7 15/16 x 5 7/8 inches (202 x 149 mm). Watermark: none. Signed, inscribed, and dated by the artist at lower left, *Ingres à Mr Norry / Pere. / rome / 1817.*

PROVENANCE: Charles Norry; Henri Rouart; Alexis Rouart; Louis-Henry Rouart; John S. Newberry, Jr.; E. V. Thaw & Co., Inc., New York.

BIBLIOGRAPHY: Lapauze 1911, pp. 165, 184, repr.; George 1934, p. 197, repr.; *Art Digest* 1950, p. 13, repr.; Naef 1977–80, II, p. 232, IV, no. 216, repr.; PML/*FR* XVIII, 1978, pp. 244, 269.

EXHIBITIONS: Paris 1924, no. 179, repr.; Paris 1934, no. 22; Detroit 1950, no. 23; Detroit 1951, no. 14, repr. as frontispiece; Pittsburgh 1951, no. 156, repr.; Cambridge 1960, no. 20, repr.; New York 1961, no. 24, repr.; Boston 1962 (no catalogue); New York PML 1981, no. 121, repr.; New York PML 1984, no. 101; Paris and New York 1993–94, no. 103., repr.

1977.37

Ingres's skill as a portrait draughtsman is demonstrated in this deft characterization of Charles Désiré Norry, who died in 1818, aged twenty-two, a year after he posed for the artist. Given his short life, not a great deal is known about the subject. The elder son of the well-known architect Charles Norry (1757–1832), Charles Désiré came to Rome to study architecture with the intention of following his father. Although not a recipient of the Prix de Rome, the young man was permitted to stay at the Villa Medici, thanks to the intervention of his father's friend Charles Thévenin, then director of the French Academy in Rome. When the elder Norry came to Rome to visit his son in 1817, both sat for Ingres. Probably at the request of M. Norry, Ingres dedicated to him his portrait of the young man. Always insightful in his portraits, Ingres revealed a certain unhappiness or dissatisfaction on the part of his sitter, whom Hans Naef characterizes as "einen seltsam unbehaglich wirkenden jungen Mann" (a strangely uneasy-looking young man) (Naef 1977–80, II, p. 232). It is likely that the younger Norry was already in ill health.

The portrait of Charles Norry, who survived his elder son by fourteen years, was in the collection of William S. Paley, New York, and recently entered the Museum of Modern Art as part of his bequest (repr. Naef 1977–80, IV, no. 215).

CDD

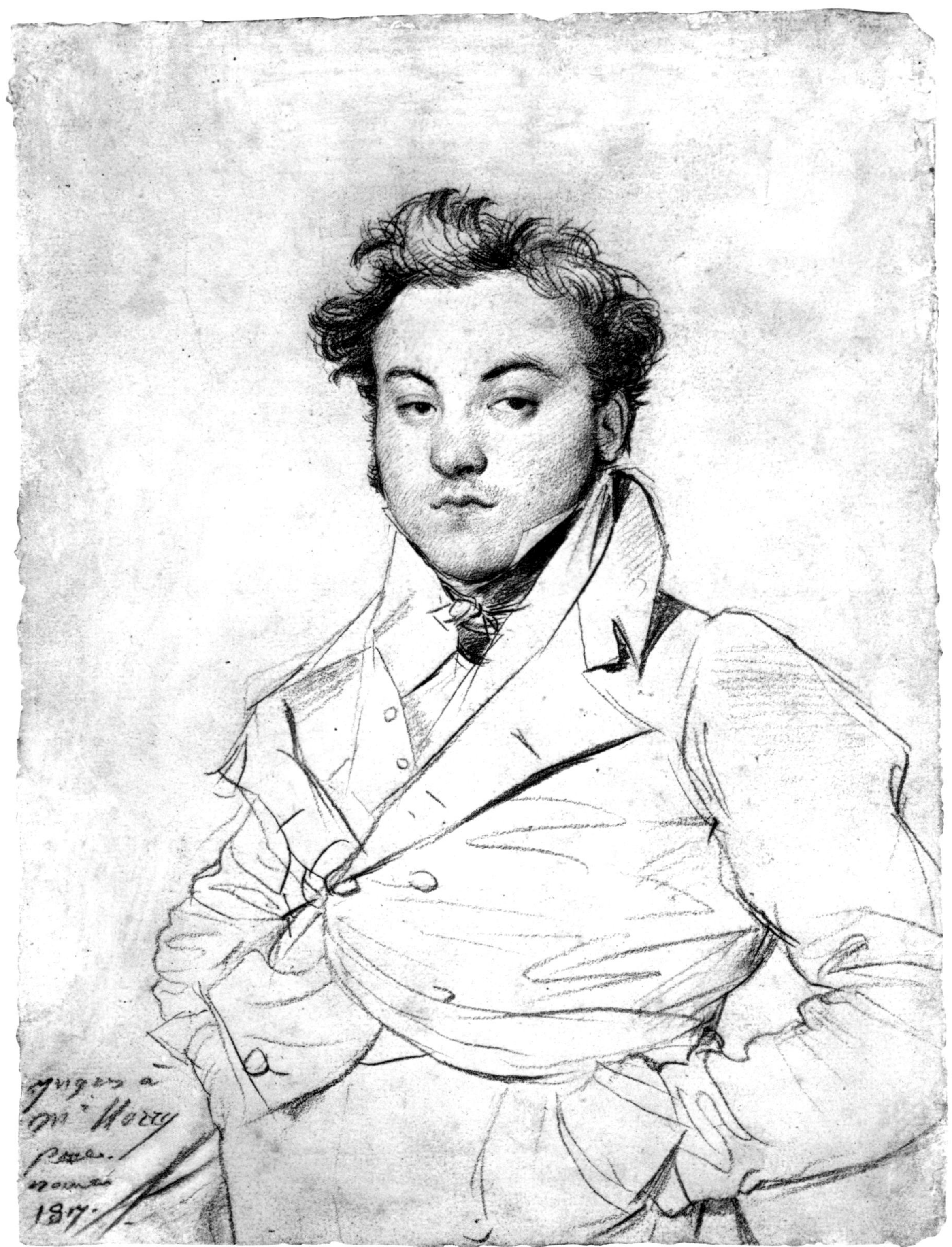
Ingres à
1817.

30

PIER LEONE GHEZZI

Rome 1674–1755 Rome

Album of Caricatures

Pen and brown ink. Sizes vary from 4 1/4 x 3 inches (108 x 76 mm) to 12 7/16 x 14 inches (368 x 479 mm). The drawings have been inserted onto the album page and pasted down. Binding: three-quarter tan leather gilt, marbled boards. Title page inscribed *DISEGNI ORIGINALI / RAPPRESENTANTI / ALCUN RITRATTI IN CARICATURA / FATTI DAL CAVALIERE / PIER LEONE GHEZZI / PITTORE ROMANO / Tomo II. / ROMA MDCCLXXX.* Some drawings inscribed by the artist, in brown ink, at lower edge with the name and description of the subject; below each drawing, in another hand, in brown ink, the name of the subject; each folio numbered in the same hand, in brown ink, above upper right corner.

48 full-length and 64 half-length caricatures, the latter mounted four to a page on folios 55–90. Folios 31, 32, 37, 38, 45, 46, 65, 66, 69–80, and 83–88 are missing, probably once including 6 full-length and 80 half-length caricatures.

PROVENANCE: eighth duke of Wellington, Stratfield Saye House, Hampshire; Robert M. Light, Boston; E. V. Thaw & Co., Inc., New York.

BIBLIOGRAPHY: PML/*FR* XIX, 1981, p. 194; Bean and Griswold 1990, under no. 68.

1978.27

Pier Leone Ghezzi was the son of the painter Giuseppe Ghezzi (1634–1721), a minor representative of the late Roman baroque. Pier Leone and the painter Antonio Amorosi (1660–1738) were both students of the elder Ghezzi at the Accademia di San Luca, where he held the position of secretary from 1678 to 1719. The younger Ghezzi began his career as an engraver, reproducing his father's paintings and making prints for book illustration. Becoming *pittore della Camera Apostolica* in 1708, he executed several papal commissions, and created frescoes (1724–33) for two ground-floor rooms in the Villa Falconieri at Frascati as well as for the Castello di Torre in Pietra. Both commissions were executed under the patronage of Cardinal Alessandro Falconieri (1657–1734), with whom Ghezzi enjoyed a long and close friendship. This relationship probably fostered Ghezzi's keen interest in antiquity (most of his drawings of antique marbles are in Codex Ottobon. 3109 at the Vatican Library). According to an inscription on a Ghezzi drawing at the British Museum (Codex f.159), both men visited the excavations at Campo Vaccino every day. Ghezzi also painted a number of altarpieces, including one in S. Salvatore in Lauro in Rome and one for the church of the Capuchins in Frascati. He also worked in precious stones and mosaic and designed architecture for festive occasions and firework displays.

Ghezzi's reputation, however, rests primarily on his talent for caricature. Many of his contemporaries, from all strata of Roman society as well as distinguished foreigners, were subject to his portrayal. The Duke of Parma honored him with the title *Conte* and Pope Clement XI (r. 1700–21) with that of *Cavaliere di Cristo*; the artist must have greatly appreciated the latter, for he always signed his drawings *Cav. Ghezzi.* A prolific draughtsman, Ghezzi filled twenty-five albums, eight of which contain caricatures (Codices Ottoboniani Latini 3112–3119, entitled *il mondo nuovo*) and are at the Vatican Library; two more are at the British Museum; and another at the Bibliothèque Nationale, Paris. The Metropolitan Museum of Art owns five Ghezzi drawings (four of them caricatures) originally from two companion volumes (Tomo I,1 and I,2) that contained eighty-nine full-page caricatures and were dismembered in the early 1970s. The three albums, including this volume, came from the collection of the dukes of Wellington. Prints after Ghezzi's caricatures were made by Arthur Pond (1705–1758), Matthaeus Oesterreich (1716–1778), and others.

The present album is practically intact. Most of the drawings date from Ghezzi's later years, about 1749 to 1754. They were placed in the volume in 1780, the date on the title page, twenty-five years after his death. Aside from their amusement value, this large group of caricatures provides a fascinating overview of contemporary Roman society, including members of the clergy, friars, abbots, and bishops as well as noblemen, artists, musicians, ordinary craftsmen, and servants. Notable among the clergymen portrayed here is the grand prior of Navarra, a Spanish knight of Malta (fol. 1); the abbate Storace, secretary to Cardinal Domenico Passionei (fol. 6); and Fra Atanasio dalla Fara Cercante, a Capuchin monk (fol. 43), of whom there is another, slightly larger, drawing in the Kupferstichkabinett, Dresden, and a print by Matthaeus Oesterreich, dated 1750. The Roman aristocracy is represented by Marchese Giacomo Massimo (1665–1751; fol. 33) and Marchese Lucatello, characterized in the artist's commentary as an eccentric (fol. 42). The architect Girolamo Teodoli (1677–1766) is shown here giving instructions to his disciple Pietruccio (fol. 27). There are also musicians, including Pasquale Bini da Pesaro (1716–1770; fol. 25), a violin virtuoso; the cellist Antonio Vandini (ca. 1690–1771); and the soprano of the papal choir, Menicuccio, who, according to the artist's commentary beneath the drawing, died in 1751 and, dressed in peacock blue and a golden cap, was buried in Chiesa Nuova with the assistance of the papal choir (fol. 20). The son of Signor Gomez (fol. 28), according to Ghezzi's inscription, is an amusing fellow who seems to be frightened by a ghost and is endowed with thin legs and tiny feet.

Ghezzi evidently was very close to people from the Marches, where his own family (his father was born in Comunanza near Ascoli-Piceno) and Cardinal Passionei, statesman and man of letters (born in Fossombrone) originated. Five members of Passionei's household are portrayed on these folios, as are Doctor Cocchi from Sant'Angelo in Vado and a painter from Ancona (not identified by name). The artist's fascination with contemporary society also led him to satirize foreign visitors, such as the duc d'Etuil, uncle of the French ambassador (fol. 26), and M. Marescial, minister of the King of Prussia (fol. 67b). The album includes very few caricatures of women: one full-length portrait of Signora Alessandra Dionisii, who, according to the inscription, died in October 1750 giving birth to a daughter (fol. 34), and six half-length figures, among them three religious women—the sister of Cardinal Sciarra and her lay sister (fols. 57a,b) and Giacinta Marescotti (1585–1640; fol. 57d), who was beatified by Benedict XIII in 1726 and canonized by Pius VII in 1807. Ghezzi's satirical bent naturally drew him to uncommon and even grotesque subjects, such as a condemned man who "died unrepentant in Rome" and a dwarf (fols. 53 and 54).

These caricatures reveal the strong influence of Ghezzi's expertise as an etcher on his drawing style. He skillfully outlined the contour of a figure with a few pen strokes and rendered the shaded parts of the figure and costume with vigorous, widely spaced parallel hatchings. These satirical drawings, together with the artist's informative autograph commentaries, make this album a historical document, a kind of "Who's Who" of mid-eighteenth-century Roman society. Ghezzi may have been inspired by some of his predecessors in this genre, such as Annibale Carracci (1560–1609) or Giuseppe Maria Mitelli (1634–1718), and he, in turn, may have had some influence on Hogarth and Rowlandson. RSK

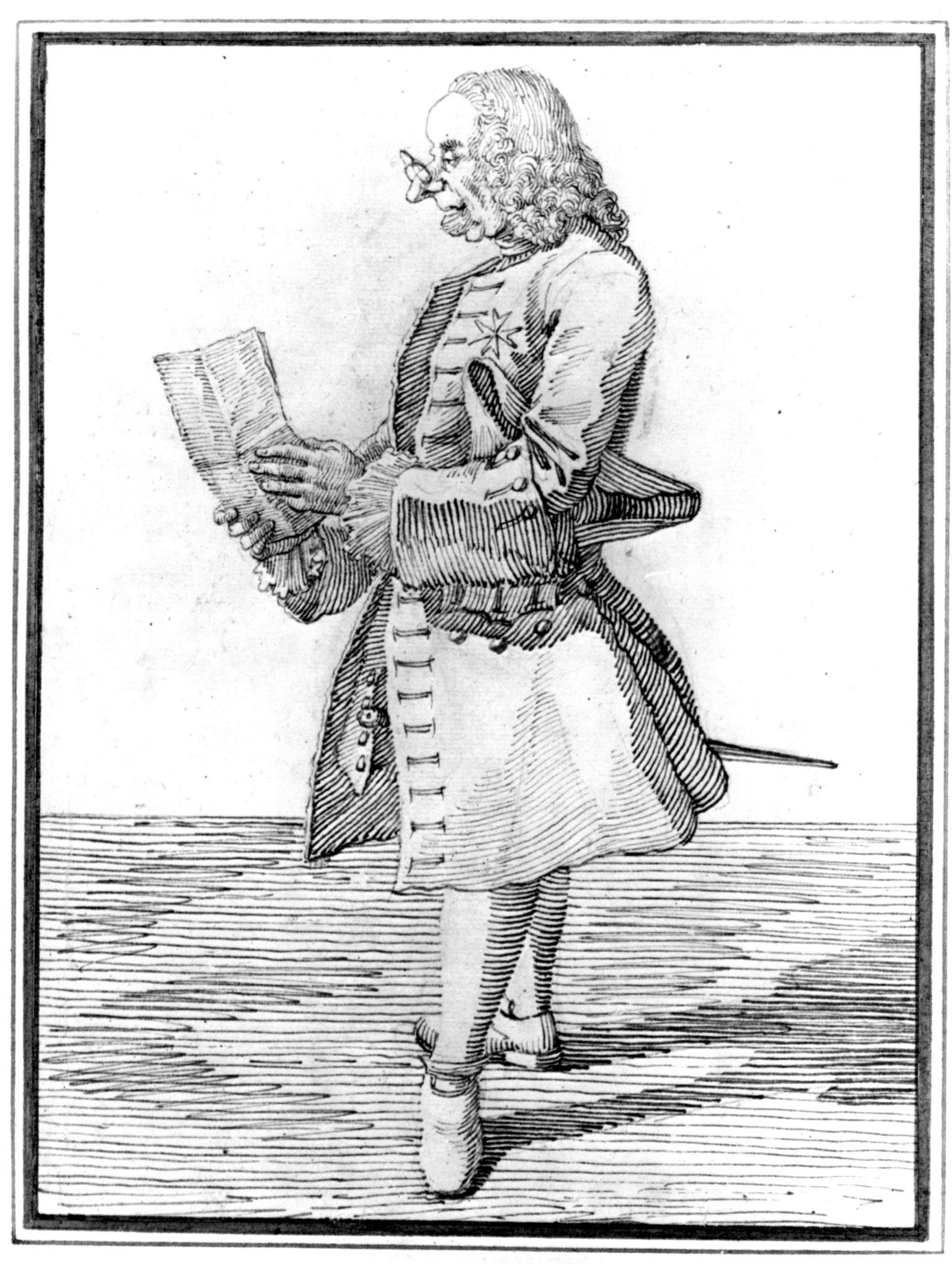

Il Gran Prior di Navarra Cav.e di Malta Spag.

30a, fol. 1

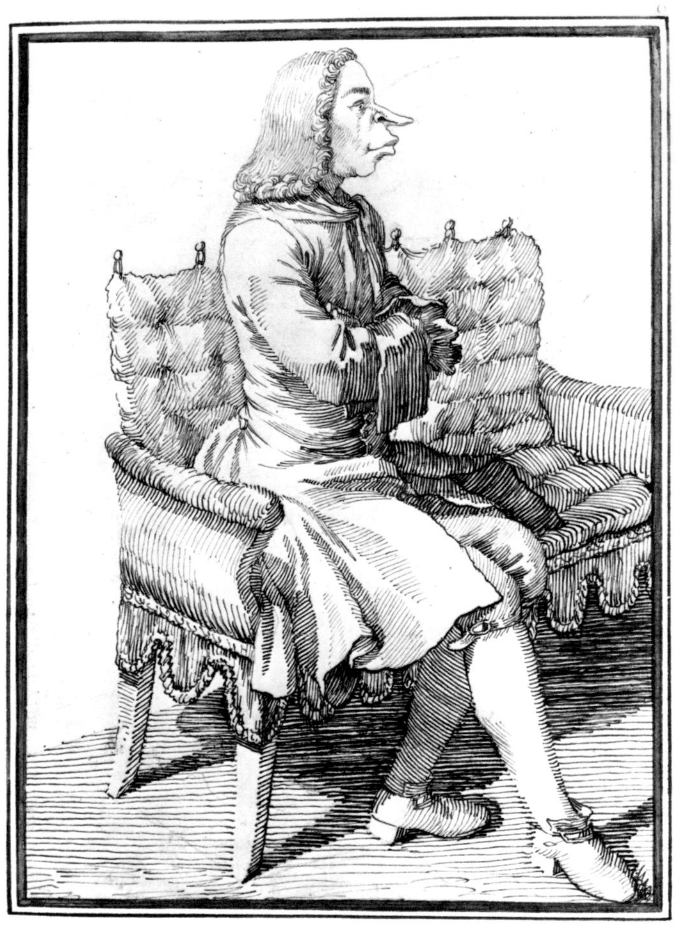

Sig.r Abb.e Storace Amanuense del Card.l Passionei

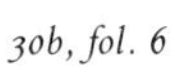

30b, fol. 6

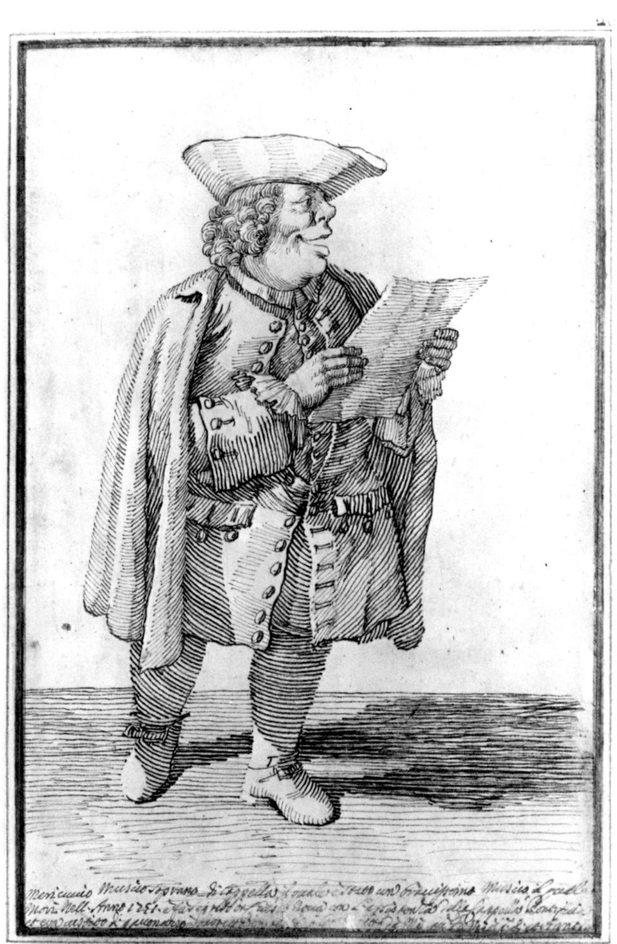

Menicuccio Musico Soprano della Capp.a Pontif.a

30c, fol. 20

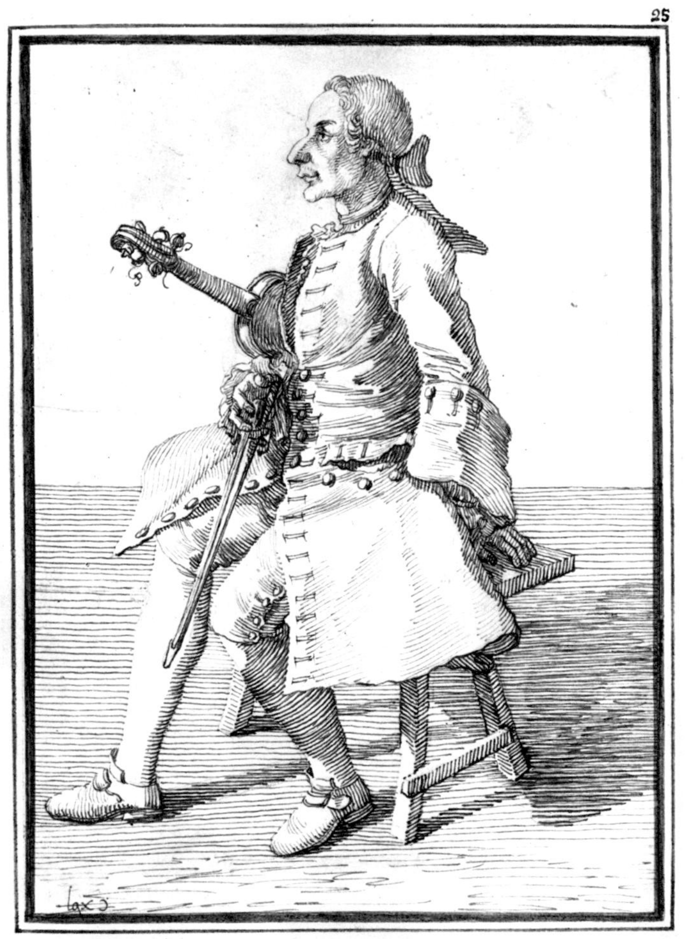

Pasquale Bini da Pesaro Suonat.^e di violino

30d, fol. 25

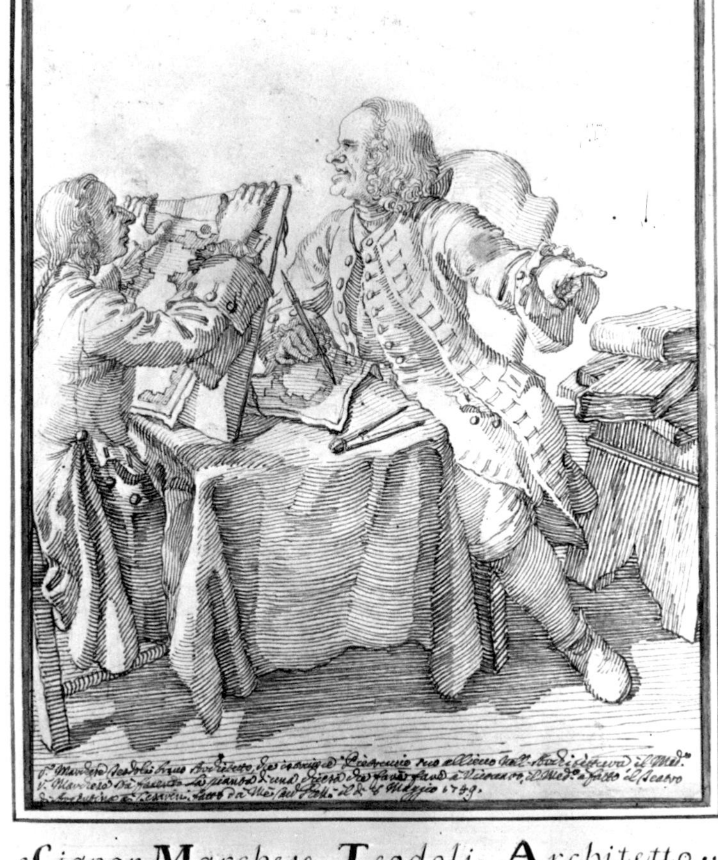

Signor Marchese Teodoli Architetto..

30e, fol. 27

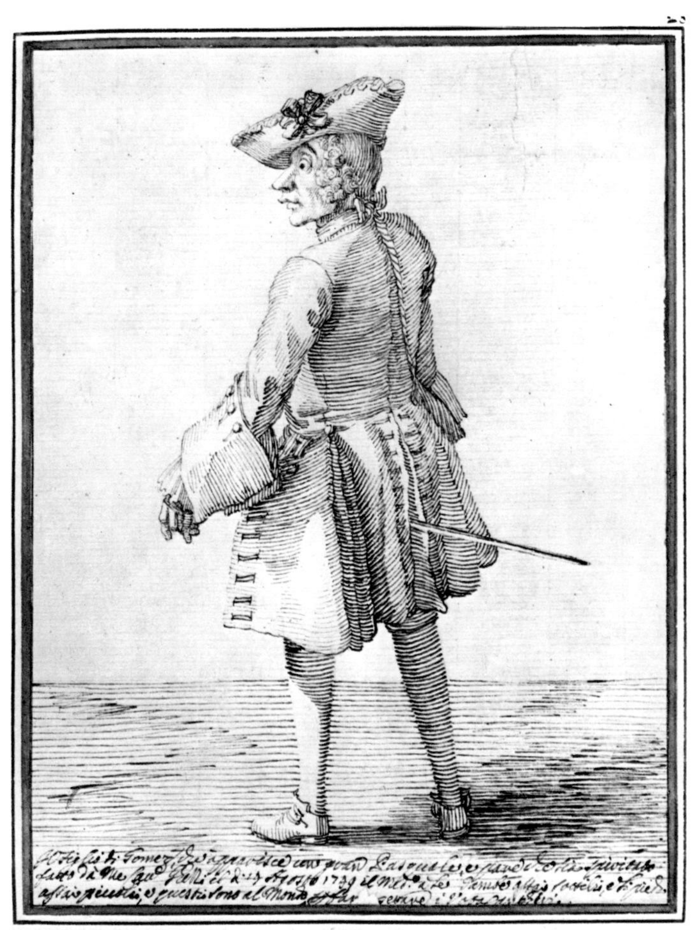

Il Figlio del Signor Gomez

30f, fol. 28

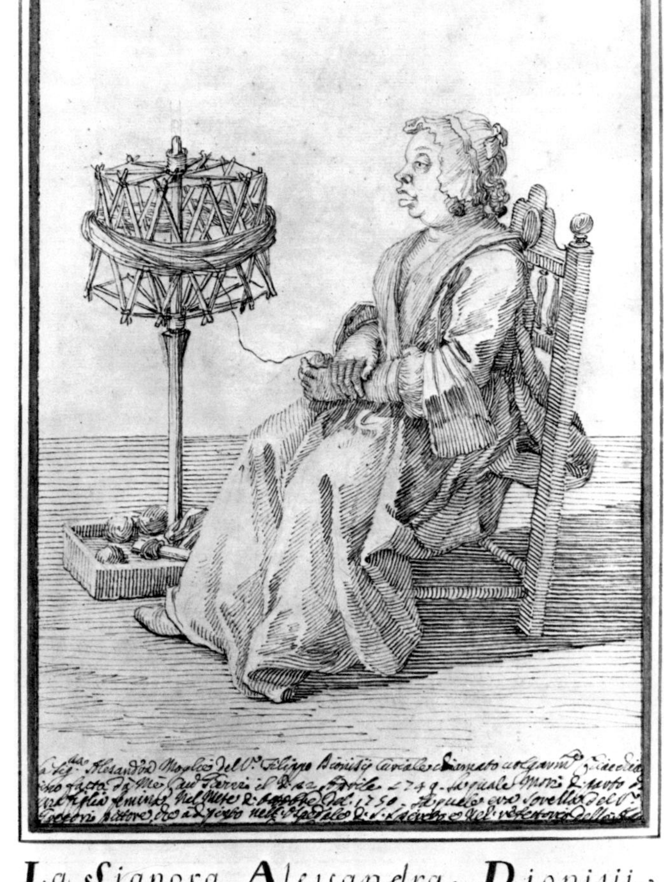

La Signora Alessandra Dionisii

30g, fol. 34

31

PIER LEONE GHEZZI

Rome 1674–1755 Rome

Self-Portrait

Pen and brown ink, over faint traces of black chalk; framing line in pen and brown ink. 7 1/2 x 5 1/8 inches (190 x 130 mm). Watermark: none visible through lining. Numbered on the old mount, at upper right in red chalk, *231*; at lower right, in pen and brown ink, *Raffaele Mengs. 28*; variously inscribed and numbered on verso.

PROVENANCE: Guglielmo Poggi (Lugt S. 2034a, his stamp on verso of drawing); Professor Jacob Isaacs; his sale, London, Sotheby's, 27 February 1964, lot 190 (as a portrait of Mengs); H. M. Calmann, London; David Daniels, New York; his sale, London, Sotheby's, 25 April 1978, lot 28, repr.; E. V. Thaw & Co., Inc., New York.

BIBLIOGRAPHY: Clark 1963, pp. 11–21; PML/*FR* XIX, 1981, pp. 194–95; Byam Shaw 1983, I, under no. 185.

EXHIBITION: Storrs 1973, no. 26.

1978.28

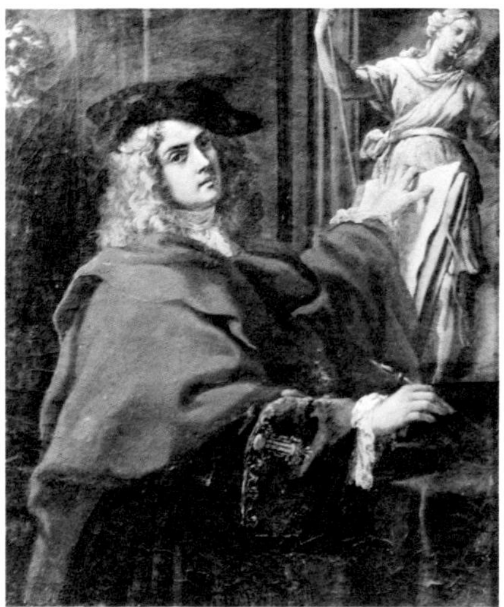

Fig. 1 Pier Leone Ghezzi, *Self-Portrait*, Galleria degli Uffizi, Florence, A399.

With its quick and deft pen strokes, this self-portrait, which once may have been part of an album, demonstrates Ghezzi's skill in capturing the salient features of a face, a technique he perfected in his many amusing, and often witty, caricatures. The drawing depicts a half-length portrait of a young man turned toward the spectator. Anthony Clark accepted the drawing as a self-portrait by Pier Leone Ghezzi (an old inscription on the drawing attributed it to Anton Raphael Mengs), but James Byam Shaw, in his discussion of Ghezzi's self-portrait in the Frits Lugt Collection, expressed doubt as to the identity of the sitter.

There are numerous Ghezzi self-portraits, among them an early frontal view that recently appeared on the art market. A closer example, however, which seems to support Clark's identification, is the painted self-portrait of the young artist at the age of twenty-eight, dated 1702, in the Uffizi (fig. 1; oil on canvas; 310 x 265 mm). In spite of the more formal appearance of the subject in cloak and hat and probably a wig, the similarity in the shape of the face, in the eyes, nose, and mouth is marked; Ghezzi also wears the tight neckband and jabot seen in this drawing. Two other self-portraits, one in the Nationalmuseum in Stockholm (654/1863; 347 x 230 mm; originally made for Nicola Pio's *Vite* and acquired by Count Tessin at the Crozat sale) and the other at the Kunsthalle in Hamburg (Inv. no. 21219b; 442 x 320 mm), dated 1717, offer a close comparison. Although executed in red chalk and showing the artist about fifteen years later, in his early forties, both drawings share the same characteristics: the serious, expressive eyes, the Roman nose, and the small, well-formed mouth.

Ghezzi also portrayed himself frequently in the manner of his satirical drawings. Among these is a self-portrait at the National Library in Valletta, Malta, where his age is incorrectly given as seventy-six years (fig. 2). (There is an almost identical version of this self-portrait at the Museo Civico in Fossombrone, near Urbino, dated 16 February 1747, on which the artist's age is correctly indicated as seventy-three years.) In the Valletta drawing, the artist is seated at a table, studying images of eyes and a nose that appear on a tablet suspended on a stand in front of him. In the inscription, he remarks that he still tries to perfect his execution of eyes and that even now, in old age, he strives to correct himself "because in this profession, the more one studies, the less one knows."

A vivid sense of the artist's physical appearance can be derived from this group of self-portraits, which span Ghezzi's lifetime. He appears among the visitors in the decoration, dated about 1724, he painted in the Salon of the Villa Falconieri at Frascati. This and two later painted self-portraits depict the aging artist: one, dated 1725, at age fifty-one, is at the Uffizi (A401); the other, dated 1747, depicting Ghezzi at seventy-three, is at the Accademia di San Luca in Rome. RSK

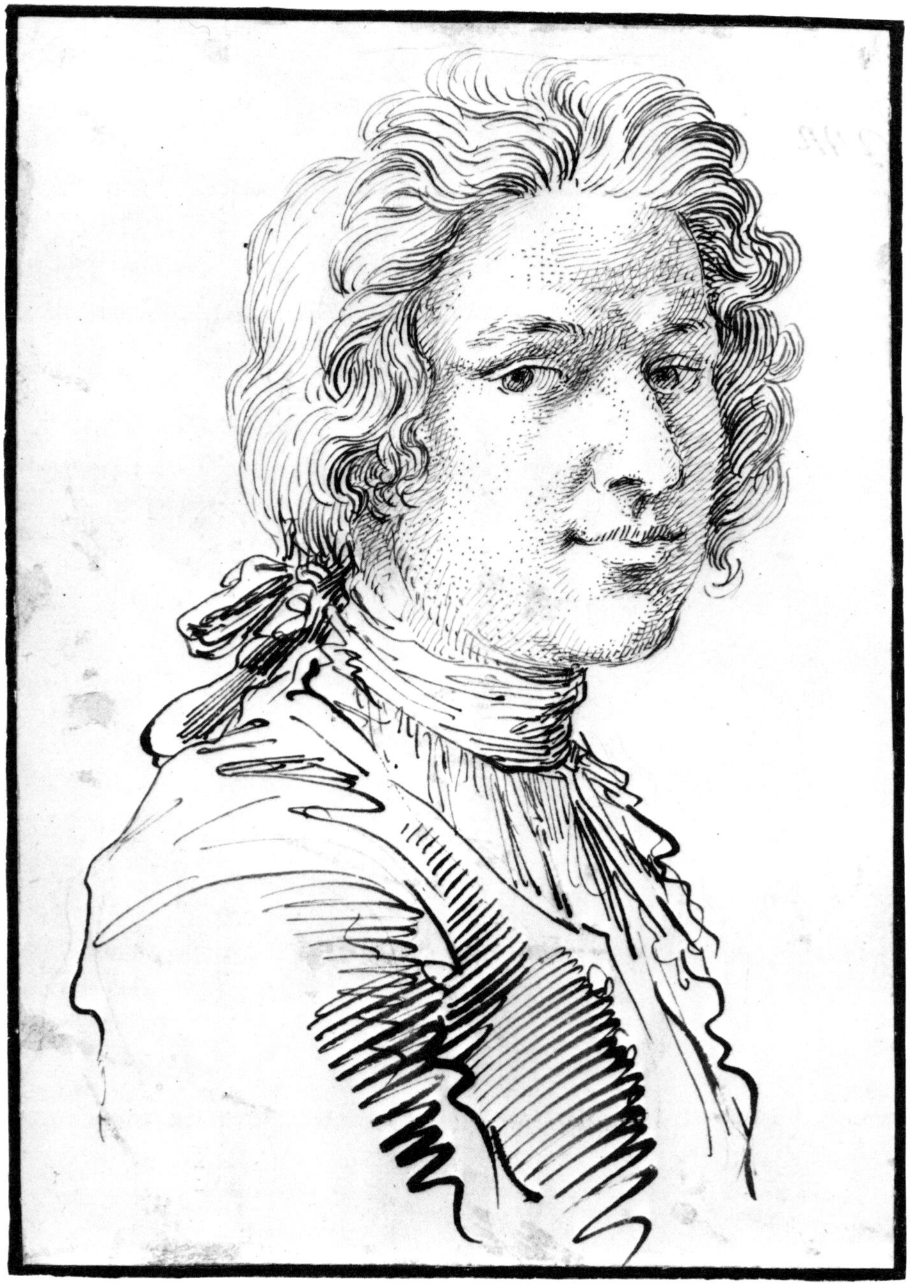

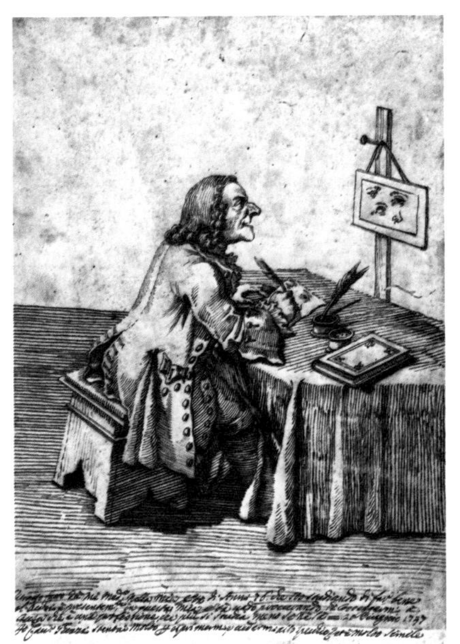

Fig. 2 Pier Leone Ghezzi, *Self-Portrait,* National Library of Malta, Valletta.

32a

NICOLA MICHETTI

1675–1759 Rome

Design for the First Machine for the Festival of the Chinea of 1731

Pen and black and brown ink, point of brush, gray and brown wash, traces of graphite; framing line in pen and brown ink. 15 3/4 x 18 9/16 inches (399 x 472 mm). Watermark: none. Signed at lower left in pen and brown ink, *NM.*

PROVENANCE: Trinity Fine Art, London; Artemis (David Carritt Limited), London.

EXHIBITION: London 1990c, no. 9, repr.

1994.6:1

Each year, on the feast of St. Peter and St. Paul, the festival of the Chinea was celebrated. During the ceremony, a member of the Colonna family presented to the pope, in the name of the king of Naples, a white horse (chinea) bearing a coffer of gold. The festival originated in the thirteenth century, when Charles of Anjou accepted the kingdom of the Two Sicilies as a fief of the church. To mark the occasion, a great pyrotechnical machine was set up in the Piazza dei SS. Apostoli, in front of the Palazzo Colonna. After the fireworks, the *macchina*, a construction of wood, canvas, and stucco, was burned to the accompaniment of recitations and music. In eighteenth-century Rome, the largest number of firework displays were organized by the contestabile Colonna, the ambassador of the king of Naples. From 1722, displays outside the Palazzo Colonna on two successive evenings became traditional, and these were held for most of the next sixty years.

From 1730, Nicola Michetti was architect to the Colonna family. John Pinto has thoroughly studied Michetti's wide range of ephemeral architecture, both secular and religious, and examined the relationship between these and the permanent structures that he designed (Pinto 1980). Michetti's formal responsibilities, like those of his predecessor, Gabriele Valvassori, would have included designing the machines for the Chinea. Based on contemporary documents and the style of the machines as recorded in prints, Pinto has determined that Michetti most likely designed six firework displays for the Chinea during the years 1731–33. In a diary entry for 1731, Pier Leone Ghezzi mentioned Michetti in a somewhat disparaging account of the fate of the first machine. The account states that the figure of Atlas misfired almost immediately, eventually burning down the entire structure as well as a nearby house (Pinto 1980, p. 309). The engraving connected with the drawing is inscribed, *Bartolomeo Poli inv. Gio Batta Sintes Incise in Rom, con lic. de Sup.* Although Michetti's name does not appear on the print, the drawing is signed with his initials, *NM*, suggesting that Michetti must have worked with the painter Poli. Pinto has observed that this design is stylistically comparable with Michetti's architecture, both in overall proportions as well as in the details.

Chinea designs such as this often incorporated familiar classical monuments. Here Hercules and Minerva are placed on pedestals flanking the crouching figure of Atlas, who supports the globe. The inscription on the print explains that the image depicts the martial feats of Charles VI in defending the Holy Roman Empire (Pinto 1980, p. 311). The drawing for the second 1731 machine, a triumphal arch that could not be set off since the first was destroyed, is at Artemis.

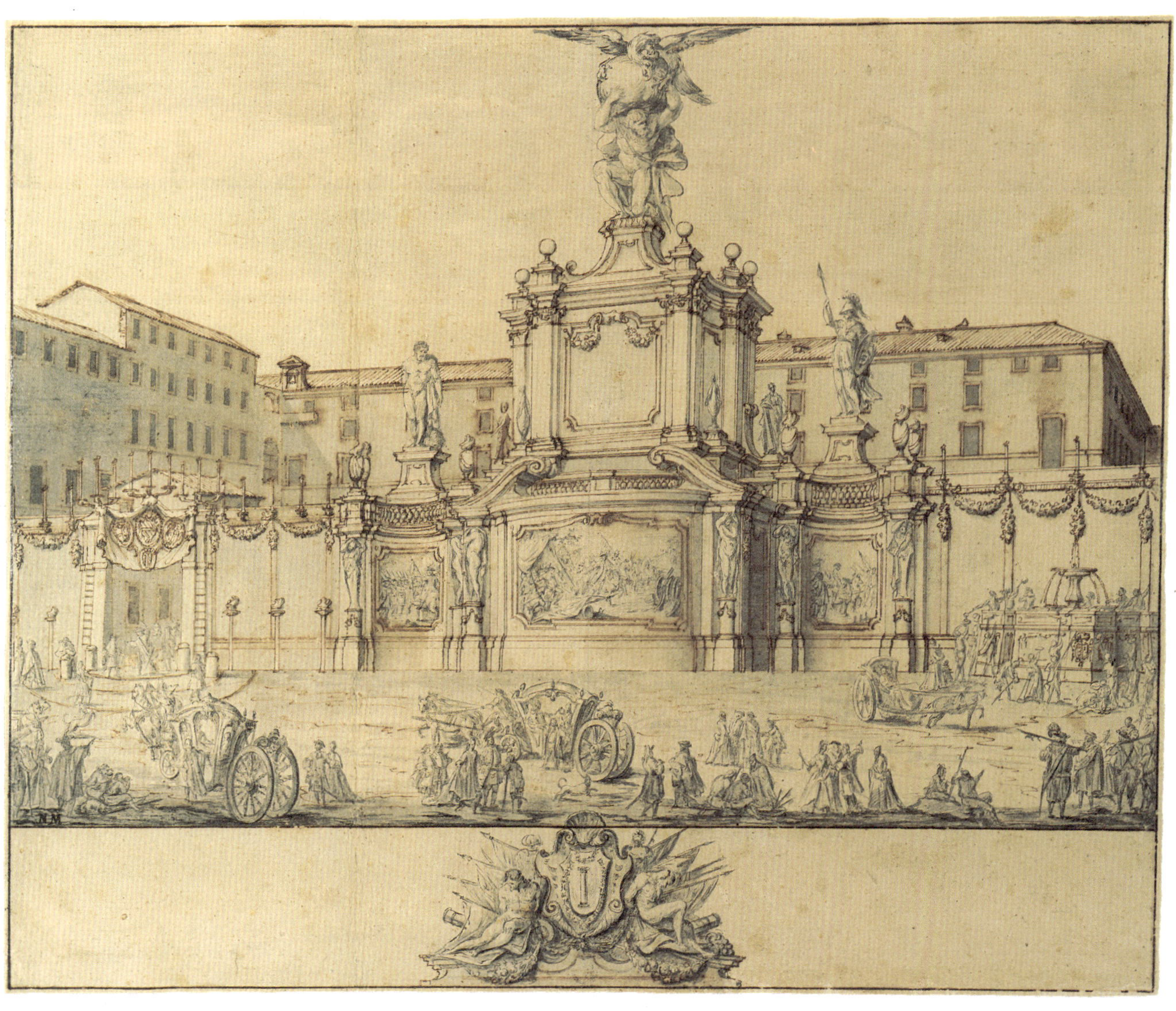

32b

Design for the First Machine for the Festival of the Chinea of 1733

Pen and brown ink, point of brush, black and gray wash, over traces of graphite; framing line in pen and brown ink. 15 11/16 x 14 13/16 inches (398 x 375 mm). Watermark: none.

PROVENANCE: Trinity Fine Art, London; Artemis (David Carritt Limited), London.

EXHIBITION: London 1990c, no. 12, repr.

1994.6:2

The machines designed for 1732 employed scenes from classical mythology to glorify the emperor Charles VI, alluding to his efforts to expand the empire and ensure peace (Pinto 1980, p. 312). These Chinea designs, prepared for 1733 (see also 32c) continued to emphasize the themes of peace and prosperity. In the first machine, Apollo with his lyre is shown seated on Mount Parnassus, accompanied by the nine Muses. In the cave below, four dancing figures are surrounded by three satyrs; two are playing music and one is drinking. The print connected with this design was made by Giovanni Battista Sintes (fig. 1).

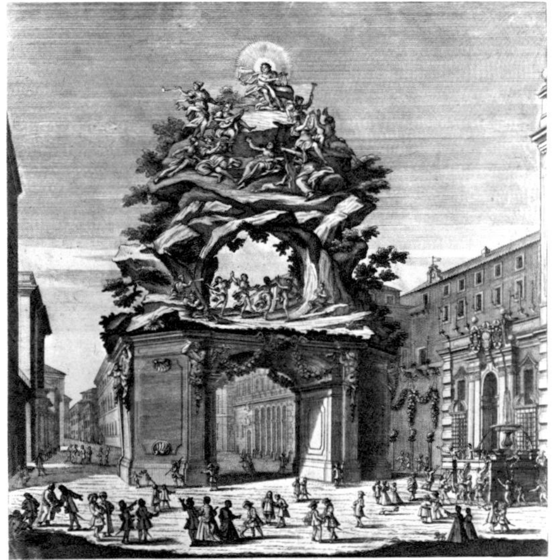

Fig. 1 Giovanni Battista Sintes, *The First Machine for the Festival of the Chinea, 1733,* The Feltrinelli Collection at The Pierpont Morgan Library, Feltrinelli 4428.

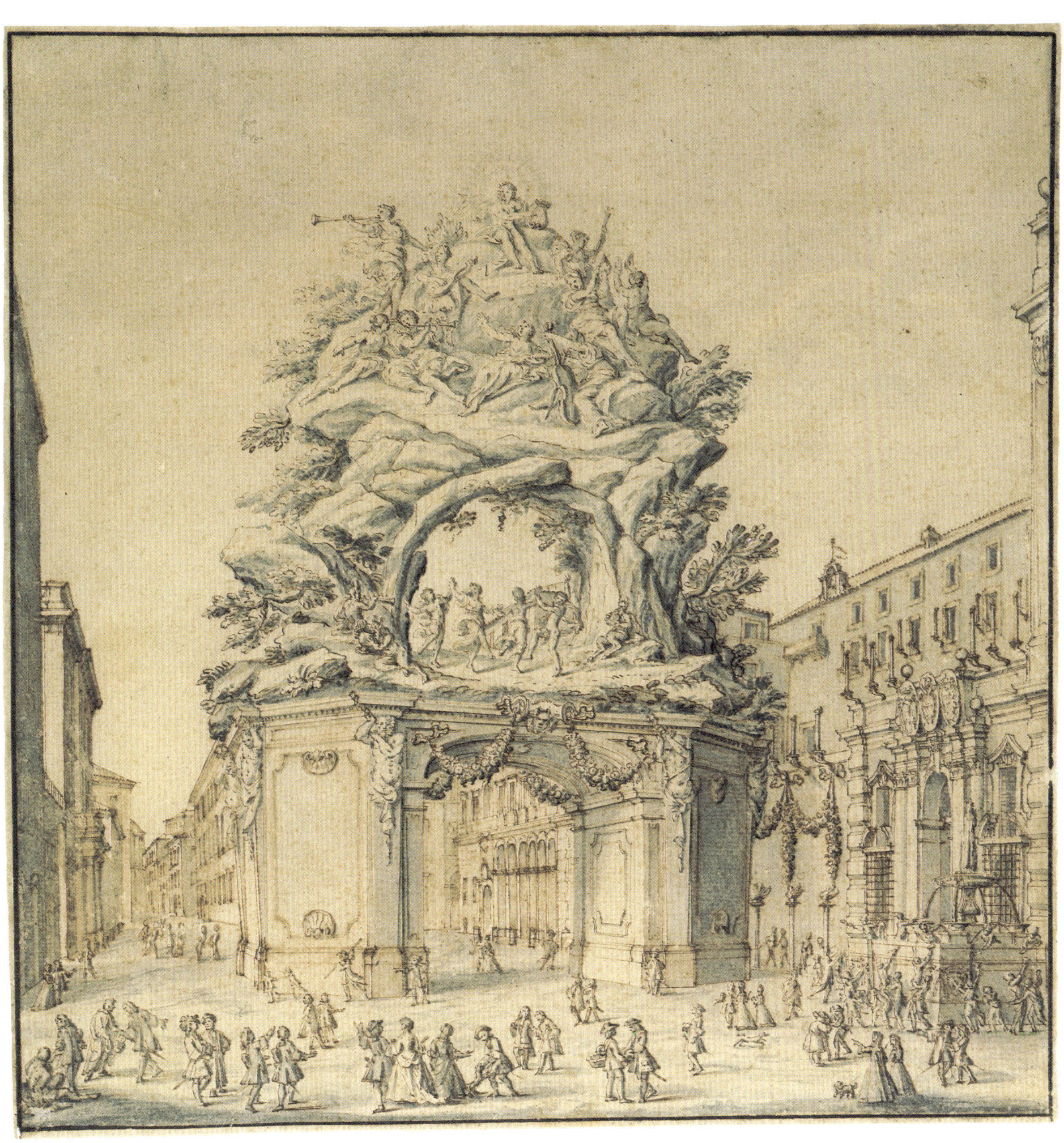

32c

Design for the Second Machine for the Festival of the Chinea of 1733

Pen and brown ink, point of brush, black and gray wash, over traces of graphite; framing line in pen and brown ink. 15 11/16 x 14 7/8 inches (398 x 377 mm). Watermark: fleur-de-lis in a circle.

PROVENANCE: Trinity Fine Art, London; Artemis (David Carritt Limited), London.

EXHIBITION: London 1990c, no. 13, repr.

1994.6:3

The second machine for 1733 (engraved by Domenico Franceschini) alludes more specifically than the first machine does to Europe's contemporary political situation—England, France, Spain, and Austria were preparing for the War of Polish Succession (Pinto 1980, p. 312). Minerva and Jupiter, seated on clouds and surrounded by armor, confer about maintaining peace; below, the manufacture of arms takes place in the forge of Vulcan. Instead of being attached to the walls of the Palazzo Colonna, the 1733 machines are freestanding, allowing for a lively foreground tableau that includes an amusing passage depicting spectators taking drinks from a fountain. This certainly must be the kind of fountain that was set up on special occasions to provide free wine for the populace as a gesture of largess (Pinto 1980, p. 306). SW

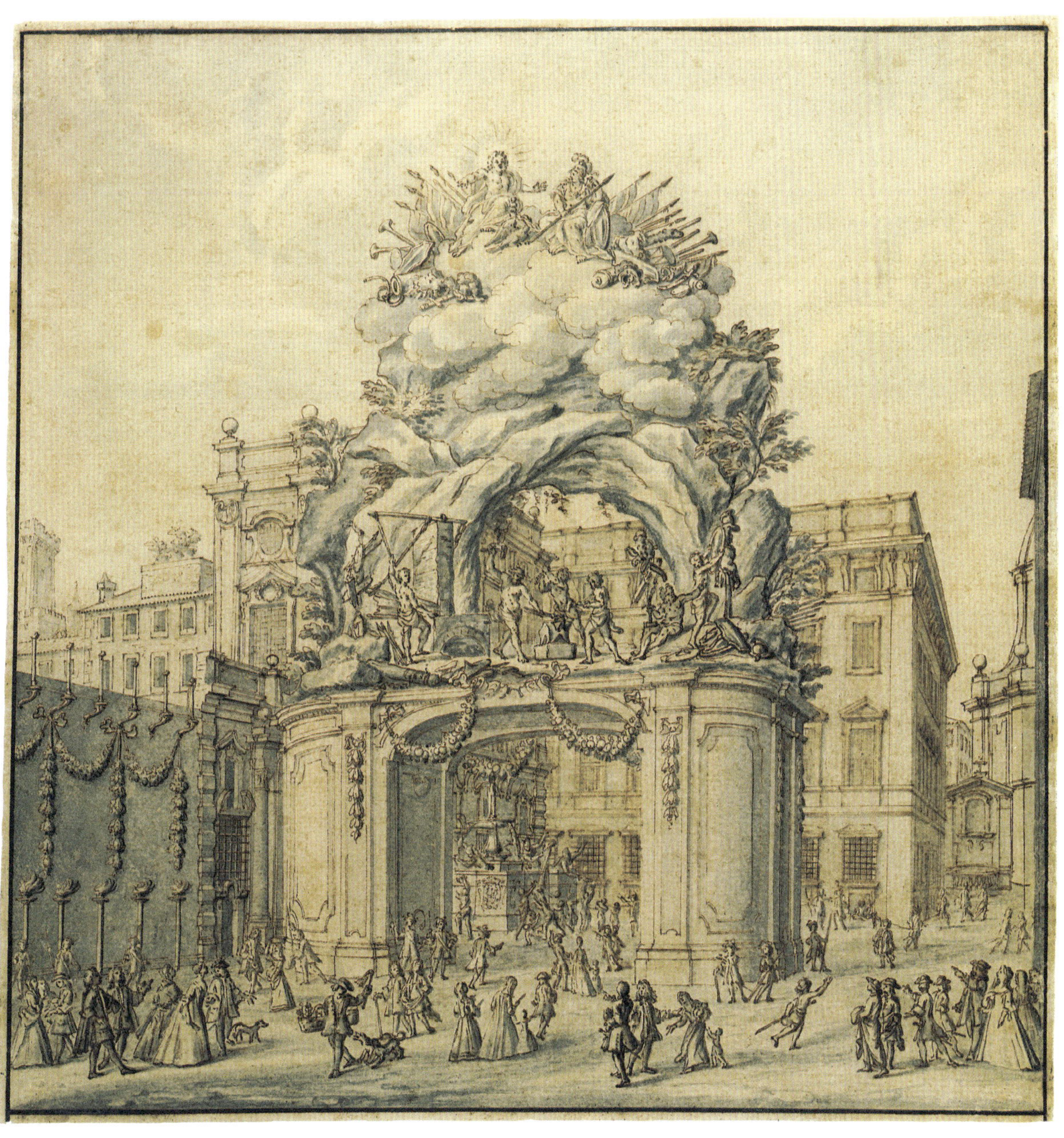

33

GIOVANNI BATTISTA PIAZZETTA

Venice 1682–1754 Venice

Study of the Virgin. *Verso:* San Luigi Gonzaga; Head of a Bearded Man

Black and some white chalk, stumped, on blue-gray paper; two horizontal folds. 18 13/16 x 14 1/4 inches (476 x 370 mm). Watermark: none.

PROVENANCE: private collection, Venice; Stephen Spector, New York; private collection, New York; Stephen Mazoh & Co., New York.

BIBLIOGRAPHY: Pallucchini 1956, p. 52, fig. 129; Mariuz 1982, no. 22b.

EXHIBITIONS: New York 1962, no. 6, repr.; Venice 1983, no. 39, repr.; Washington 1983–84, no. 23, repr.

1991.10

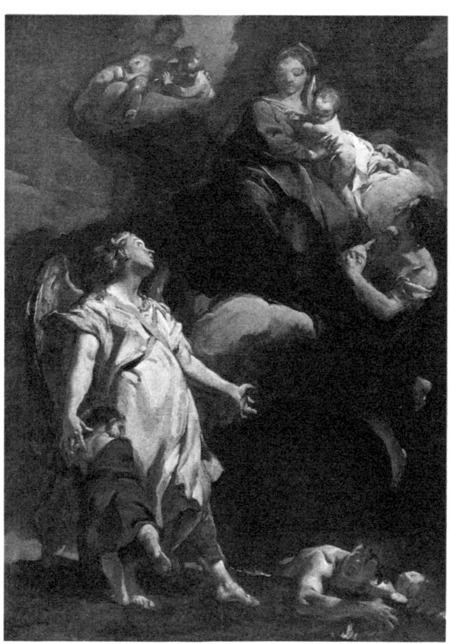

Fig. 1 Giovanni Battista Piazzetta, *Virgin and Child,* Los Angeles County Museum of Art, 46.30.

In 1956, Rodolfo Pallucchini connected this drawing with the Virgin in an altarpiece by Piazzetta that showed her appearing to the guardian angel (Pallucchini 1956). Painted for the Scuola dell'Angelo Custode in Venice, Piazzetta's work was not accepted by the scuola but was acquired instead by Zaccaria Sagredo (1653–1729). A fragment of the altarpiece is preserved in Detroit, and a *modello* for it is in the Staatliche Kunstsammlungen Kassel (Pallucchini 1956, figs. 16 and 17; Mariuz 1982, nos. 22 and 24). An oil sketch in the Los Angeles County Museum of Art (fig. 1) comes closest to the composition of the altarpiece, which we know from a print by Giuseppe Wagner (inscribed with Piazzetta's name as inventor). Generally dated ca. 1718–19, the altarpiece cannot have been executed later than 1720 since that was the year Sebastiano Ricci painted his *Angelo Custode,* which was accepted by the scuola in place of Piazzetta's.

The serenity that Piazzetta has captured in his depiction of the Virgin makes this a very compelling image. Unfinished details, such as her hand, clearly reveal one stage of the artist's development of her attitude and pose. Piazzetta made use of the figures of the Virgin and Child on at least two later occasions: in an altarpiece in San Filippo, Cortona, and one in Meduno, both executed between 1739 and 1744 (Pallucchini 1956, figs. 97 and 96; Mariuz 1982, nos. 106 and 108). George Knox has connected this drawing with these later commissions and tentatively identified it as a study for the Cortona altarpiece (Venice 1983, no. 39). Peter Dreyer, who has thoroughly studied the drawing, has suggested that it might be connected with the earlier works. Since all the paintings show the figure in reverse, he speculates that Piazzetta may have begun with this drawing, reversed it during his preparations, and worked with a later, reversed study of the Virgin thereafter. Moreover, he points out that the inclination of the Virgin's head, as well as her expression, corresponds most closely to the oil sketch in Los Angeles. Certainly the fluid movement of the arm and wrist also seem more evocative of Piazzetta's early conception.

The half-length study of San Luigi Gonzaga on the left side of the verso is probably, as Knox has observed, a study for a painting in a private collection, Cologne, engraved by Marco Pelli (Mariuz 1982, nos. 73 and 73a). The figure, which was reproduced in reverse in Knox's catalogue, is in the same direction as that in the painting. The study of a bearded man on the right side of the verso has not yet been connected to any other work. SW

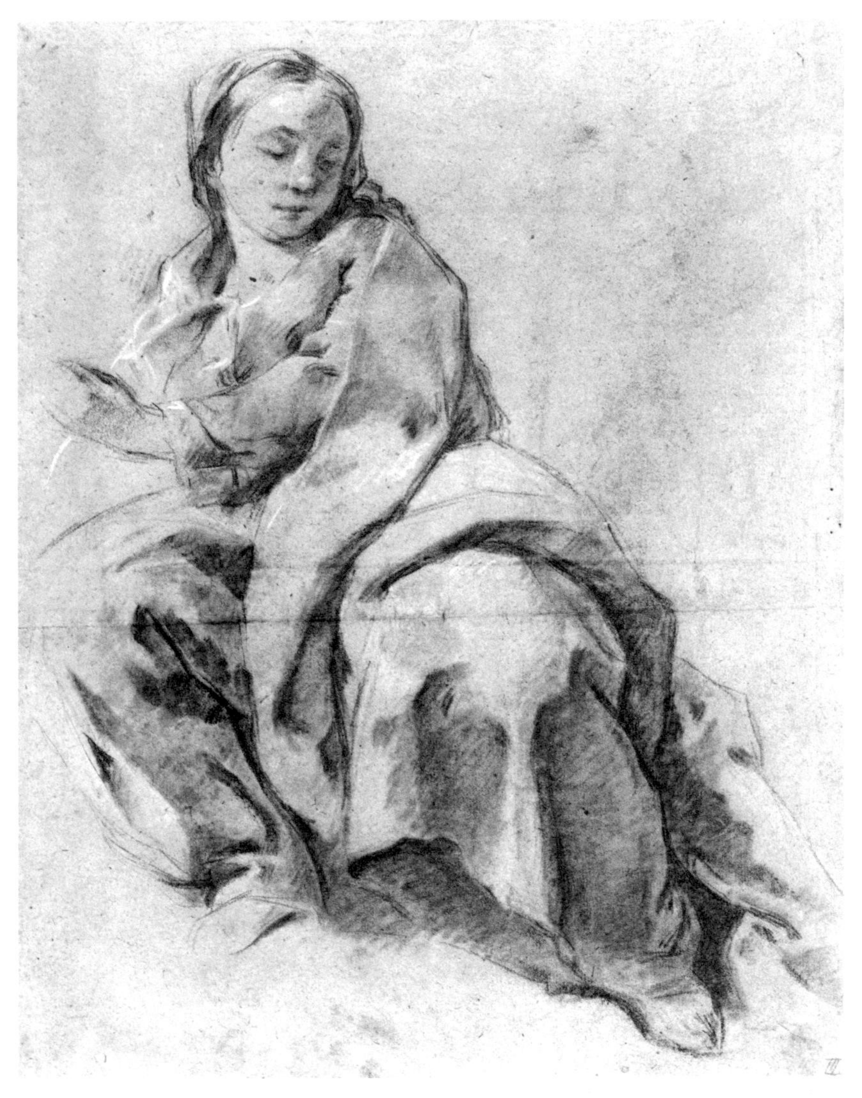

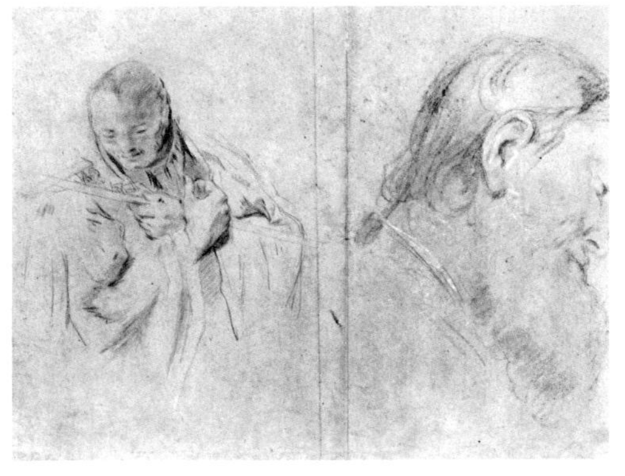

34a

GIOVANNI PAOLO PANNINI

Piacenza 1691–1765 Rome

Classical Ruins, with Antique Statues and Eight Figures

Pen and black ink, watercolor, over black chalk. 14 x 9 3/8 inches (356 x 238 mm). Watermark: none visible through lining. Signed with initials at lower left, in pen and black ink, *IPP*.

PROVENANCE: Pierre-Jean Mariette (Lugt 1852); Sir Geoffrey Harmsworth; sale, London, Sotheby's, 25 March 1982, one of two in lot 79.

BIBLIOGRAPHY: London 1982, no. 16, p. 3, repr. (in color), front cover; PML/*FR* XX, 1984, pp. 226–27, 286, fig. 24.

EXHIBITION: Montreal 1993, no. 2, repr.

1982.18:1

Pannini, who went to Rome about 1711, was professor of perspective at the French Academy, a post he held for more than thirty years until his death in 1765. It is apparent from their comparable size, as well as the mount and mark of Pierre-Jean Mariette (1694–1774), that this drawing and the following one were made as a pair, probably at Mariette's request. Mariette's mount is recognizable by its blue color, gold borders, and ruled black lines embellished with an open cartouche in which the collector inscribed the artist's name. A connoisseur of the first rank, Mariette owned, according to Chennevières, at least twenty-six drawings by Pannini (Mariette 1851–60, IV, p. 79 n.1). In the *Correspondance des directeurs de l'Académie de France à Rome*, Natoire makes reference to drawings by Pannini that he is sending to Mariette in care of Marigny (8 July 1761 and 14 October 1761).

Pannini's talent lay in his skill as a perspective draughtsman and in his seemingly limitless capacity to arrange and rearrange Roman monuments into pictures of great charm. In the present drawing, Pannini placed within the ruins of an antique palace or basilica two well-known antique statues, *Silenus with the Infant Bacchus*, now in the Louvre, and the *Nile*, in the Vatican Museum, who holds a cornucopia and rests his lower left arm on the sphinx. The putti on the *Nile* were not repaired until shortly before 1774. Two drawings in the Graphische Sammlung Albertina, Vienna, are virtual replicas of these drawings (fig. 1; Inv. nos. 2941–42). There are, however, slight differences in the coloration of the sheets, and the Albertina drawings are signed *Pannini*. Since the quality of all four drawings is equally high, it must be assumed that Pannini sometimes repeated his most successful compositions, probably at the request of a friend or patron.

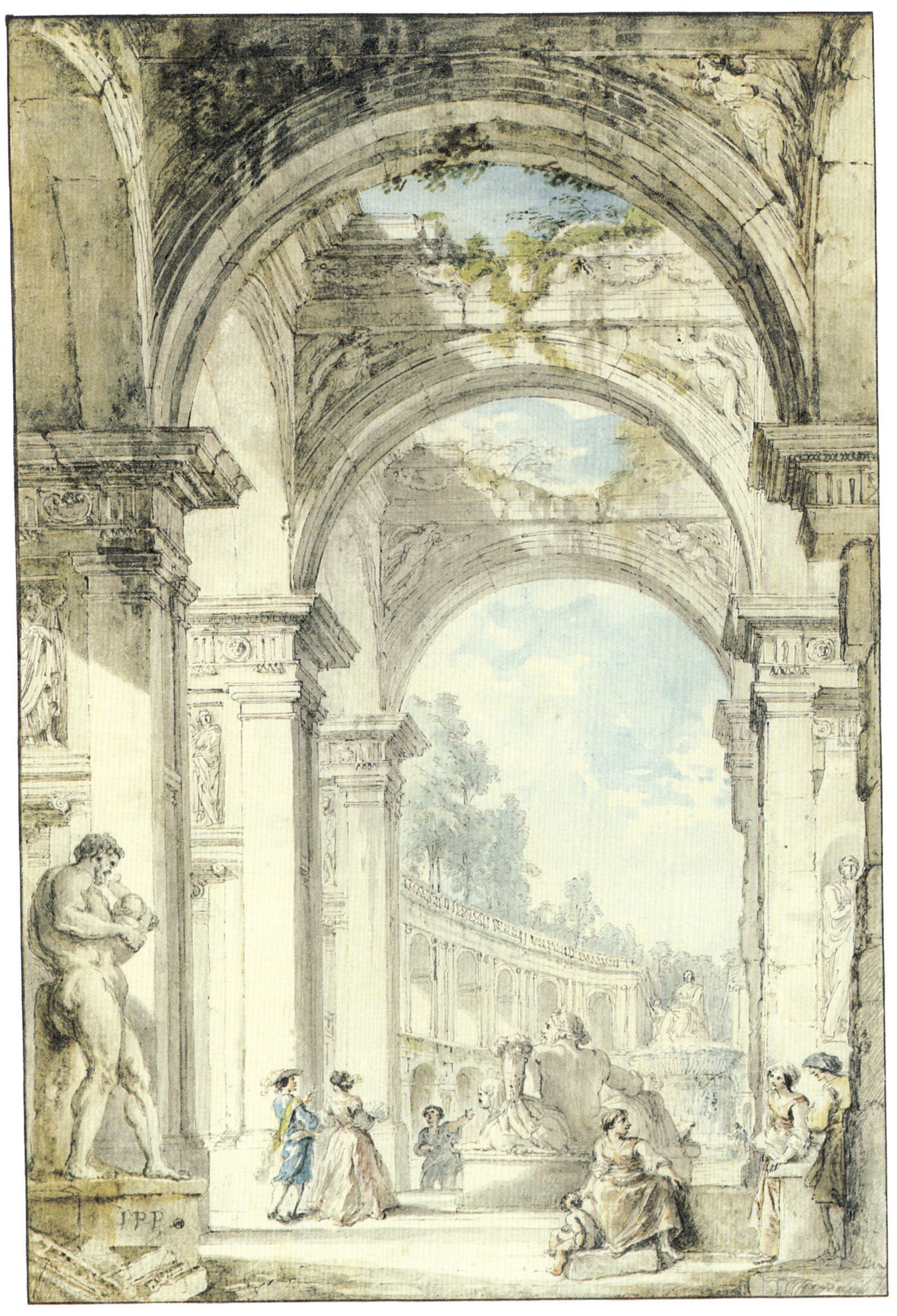

85

34b

Classical Ruins with Twelve Figures

Pen and black ink, watercolor, over black chalk. 13 7/8 x 9 3/8 inches (352 x 238 mm). Watermark: none visible through lining. Signed with initials at lower left, in pen and black ink, *IPP*.

PROVENANCE: Pierre-Jean Mariette (Lugt 1852); Sir Geoffrey Harmsworth; sale, London, Sotheby's, 25 March 1982, one of two in lot 79.

BIBLIOGRAPHY: London 1982, p. 3, repr. (in color), back cover; PML/*FR* XX, 1984, pp. 226–27, 286.

EXHIBITION: Montreal 1993, no. 3, repr.

1982.18:2

The striking motif of figures standing behind a cloth—in this case a bright blue and white one—draped over a balustrade appears in a number of paintings by Pannini. On the right, he included the sarcophagus, decorated with acanthus scrollwork and putti, of Constantina, daughter of Constantine I, from S. Costanza, Rome (Vatican Museum). The statue of Apollo Citharoedos in the center appears in another Pannini drawing in the Louvre (Inv. no. 6724; Paris, Musée du Louvre, Piacenza, Museo Civico, Braunschweig, Herzog Anton Ulrich Museum, *Pannini*, catalogue by Michael Kiene, 1992–93, no. 48). SW

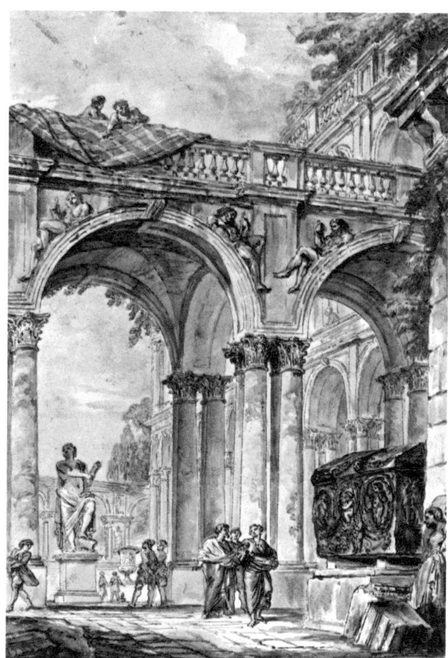

Fig. 1 Giovanni Paolo Pannini, *Antique Hall in Ruins,* Graphische Sammlung Albertina, Vienna, Inv. 2941.

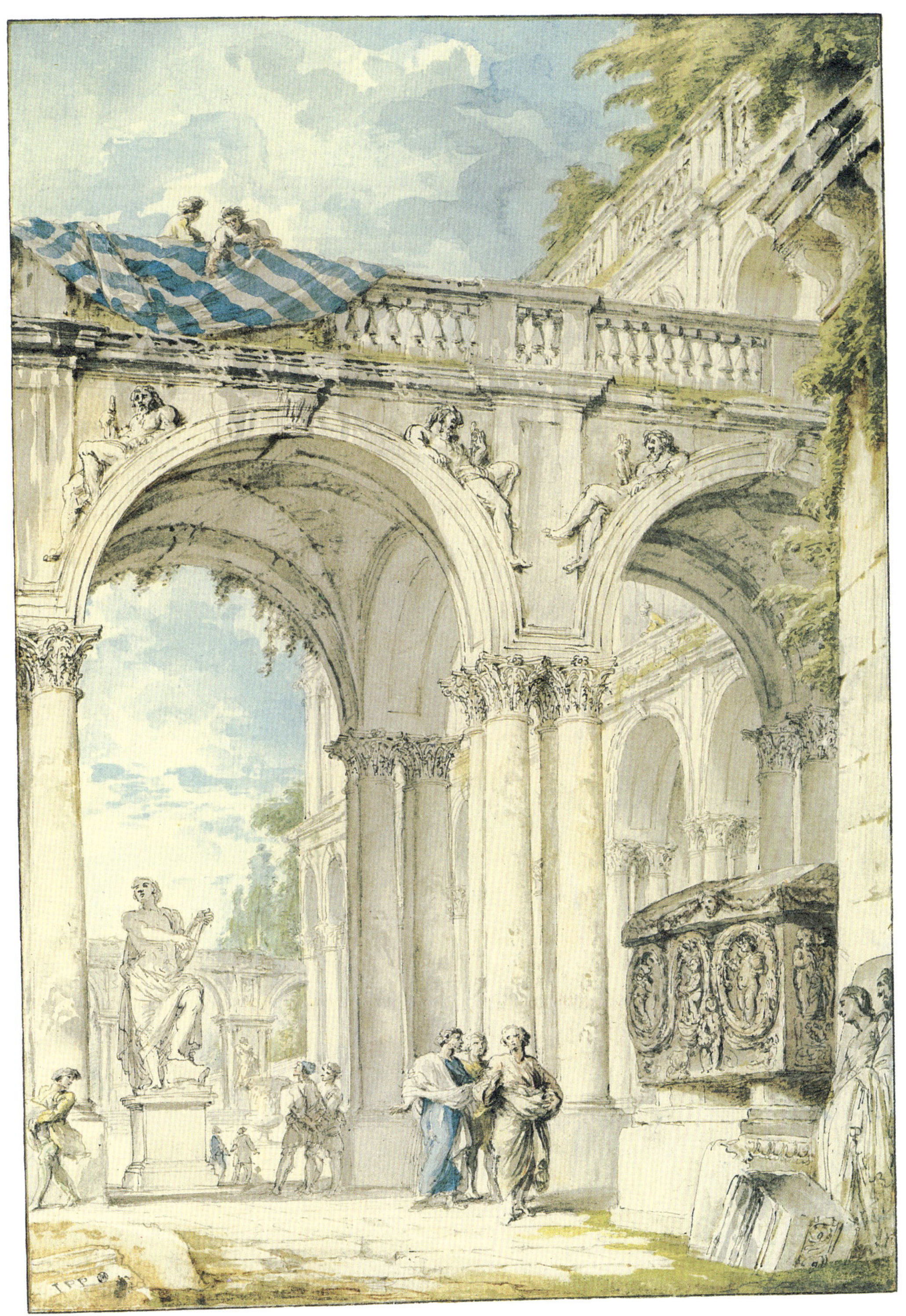

35

ANTONIO CANAL, called CANALETTO
Venice 1697–1768 Venice

Capriccio with a Round Tower and Ruins by the Lagoon

Pen and brown ink, gray and some brown wash over traces of black chalk; double-ruled border in pen and brown ink. 10 15/16 x 16 7/8 inches (277 x 430 mm). Watermark: letters *IV* (cf. Churchill 425). Signed(?) by the artist at lower left, in pen and brown ink, *Antonio Canal del.*

PROVENANCE: marquis of Landsdowne; his sale, London, Sotheby's, 25 March 1920, lot 14, repr. (to Ellis & Smith for £200); private collection, France; private collection, Washington, D.C.; E. V. Thaw & Co., Inc., New York.

BIBLIOGRAPHY: Constable and Links 1976, I, no. 806, repr., II, pp. 680–81; PML/*FR* XX, 1984, pp. 228–29, 246.

1983.76

This exceptional work, fully realized in pen and two shades of wash, provides a sweeping vista that leads the eye from the sparkling detail of the tower and ruins in the foreground, picked out by Canaletto's meticulous penwork and toned by transparent gray wash along with a little brown wash for added contrast and richness, to the lagoon in the middle ground, where the bridge recedes into the distant horizon. Another imaginary view with a similar conception of space is the *Lagoon Capriccio*, a drawing in The Metropolitan Museum of Art (repr. New York 1971, no. 155). The Metropolitan Museum *Capriccio* is related to a 1740 painting in the Uffizi, in which many of the same elements appear in reverse. No related painting is known for the present drawing, but it was engraved by Fabio Berardi in a series of six without title and published by Giuseppe Wagner. The engraving, inscribed *Lieto è il nocchier quando ritorna in porto*, is in reverse and differs from the drawing in a number of respects (Constable and Links 1976, I, no. 806). Another drawing engraved in the same series, *Imaginary Composition: A Church on a Hill, a Lagoon in the Distance*, is preserved in the Victoria and Albert Museum, London (Constable and Links 1976, I, no. 805).

CDD

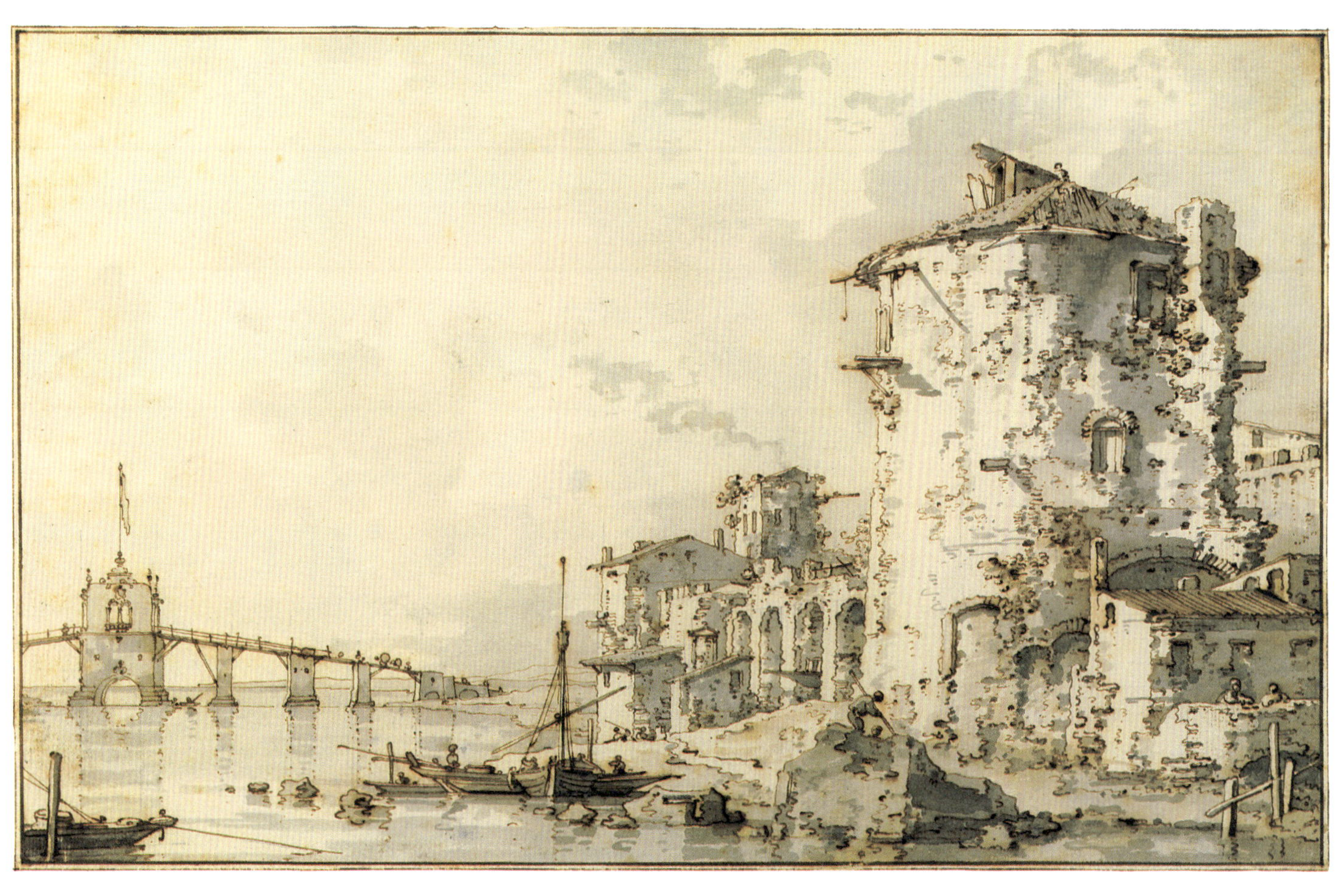

36

LUIGI VALADIER

Rome 1726–1785 Rome

Inkstand in Rococo Style

Pen and brown ink, brown wash, some red wash, over pencil; center measured in pencil with additional horizontal divisions to lay out the design. 14 3/4 x 20 5/8 inches (375 x 524 mm). Watermark: fleur-de-lis in a circle. Signed and dated at lower left, in pen and brown ink, *Luigi Valadier Fecit Roma 1764.*

PROVENANCE: Giuseppe Valadier (Luigi's son); presumably Giuseppe Spagna (who, with his son Pietro Paolo, took over the Valadier workshop); art market, Rome, ca. 1880 (when the firm, then run by Spagna's principal assistant, Giuseppe Salvi, went out of business); private collection, Europe; Artemis (David Carritt Limited), London.

BIBLIOGRAPHY: *Valadier, Three Generations of Roman Goldsmiths*, repr. in advertisement in *Apollo*, May 1991; Fuhring 1991, p. 473.

EXHIBITION: London 1991, no. 12, repr. (in color) (album no. 53a).

1991.15

Luigi Valadier, son of Andrea Valadier (1695–1759), was the most important Italian goldsmith of French descent of his time. The great diversity of his decorative work can be studied in his lively drawings, which tell a great deal not only about the historical development of decorative objects but also about the way in which the people who owned them lived. This drawing, signed and dated 1764, was made the year after Luigi and his less talented brother, Giovanni, had set up separate workshops. Luigi moved to 89 via del Babuino, where his workshop flourished, eventually sustaining some 180 employees (see London 1991, p. 35).

The album from which this drawing was removed was presumably compiled by Giuseppe Spagna after he purchased the Valadier workshop in 1817. As the 1991 catalogue notes, the works signed by Luigi were executed in pen and brown ink on high-quality Dutch export paper, which the artist used when he worked in France. The influence of French rococo design on Valadier is evident in a number of drawings, including the present one. As Peter Fuhring has pointed out, this is a copy of the *Ecritoire en porcelaine*, etched by Gabriel Huquier after Juste-Aurèle Meissonier (*Œuvres*, pl. G-42 [see below]), to which Valadier added details such as the lids on the inkwells and the candelabra. Fuhring also observes that the shell-shaped feet were based on Meissonier's silver candlestick of 1728, adding that *Les Œuvres de Meissonier, la plûpart utiles à nos Dessinateurs* (*Discours sur la nécessité de l'étude de l'architecture*, Paris [1754]) was a recommended text at the art school of Jacques François Blondel, where Valadier might have studied. Valadier's additions enhance the exuberant impact of the design, which is strengthened by the intensity of the iron gallnut as well as the fact that it presses outside the framing lines. Here the bell is placed behind the central inkpot, which holds a sponge and has a perforated rim for the quills, both of which appear in a later inkstand probably commissioned by Pius VI around 1775 (London 1991, no. 18). SW

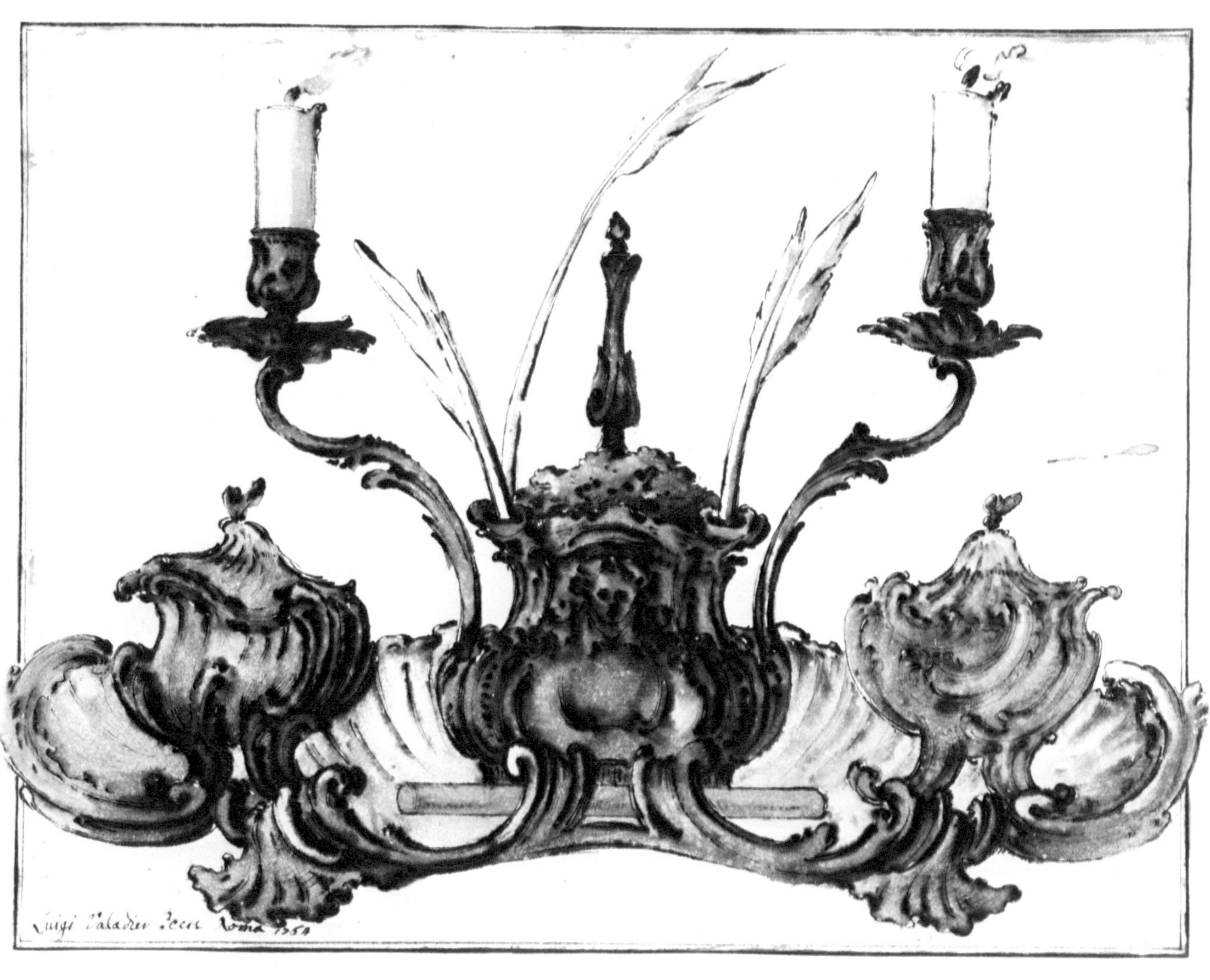

37

FRANCESCO CASANOVA

London ca. 1732/33–1802 Brühl (Vienna)

Pastoral Landscape

Brush and brown wash, over black chalk. Full sheet: 18 1/2 x 23 5/8 inches (471 x 600 mm). Design area: 15 5/16 x 20 inches (387 x 509 mm). Watermark: none. Ruled decorative border in pen and brown ink, washed in green, drawn by the artist.

PROVENANCE: Mme Meyer, Paris (according to Robert Manning); Robert and Bertina Suida Manning, New York; E. V. Thaw & Co., Inc., New York.

BIBLIOGRAPHY: Minneapolis 1961, under no. 100.

EXHIBITION: New York 1971, no. 285, repr.

1982.90

Although born in London, Francesco, the younger brother of the famous Giacomo Casanova, was raised in Venice, where he received his earliest artistic training in the workshop of Francesco Guardi. Somewhat later, he studied in Florence with Francesco Simonini, best known for his copies of the battle paintings of Jacques Courtois, called il Borgonone. Eventually, Casanova traveled to Paris, where he worked with Charles Parrocel. There, he had a huge success with his first exhibition in 1761 and was admitted to the Académie Royale in 1763. He lived in Paris for many years, later traveling to Dresden and Vienna, where he died.

Although drawings by Casanova are scarce in other major European collections, there is a fairly large concentration of them in the Albertina, Vienna. While the majority are battle scenes done in the manner of Jacques Courtois, the group also contains a number of pastoral subjects, comparable to the present drawing, with farm animals, most of which were also executed in chalk, pen, and wash. These pastorals suggest the influence of seventeenth-century Dutch art. In this drawing, the example of Nicolaes Berchem is particularly apparent in the feathery chalk line that contrasts with the transparent, atmospheric brown wash.

The green wash bordering band, or autograph "mount," indicates that the landscape was executed as an end in itself rather than as a preparatory study for a picture—a practice that became increasingly popular during the eighteenth century. This is one of a pair of pastoral drawings by Casanova; the other is in the Manning Collection (fig. 1). Both are exceptionally large compared with other drawings by the artist. CDD

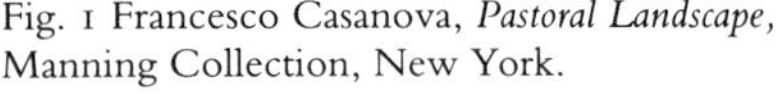

Fig. 1 Francesco Casanova, *Pastoral Landscape,* Manning Collection, New York.

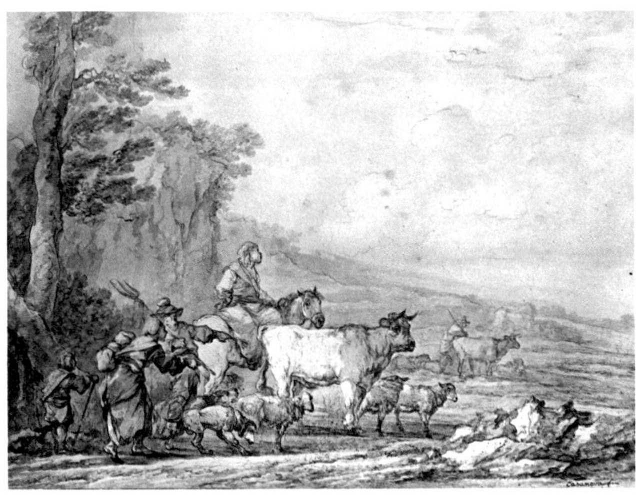

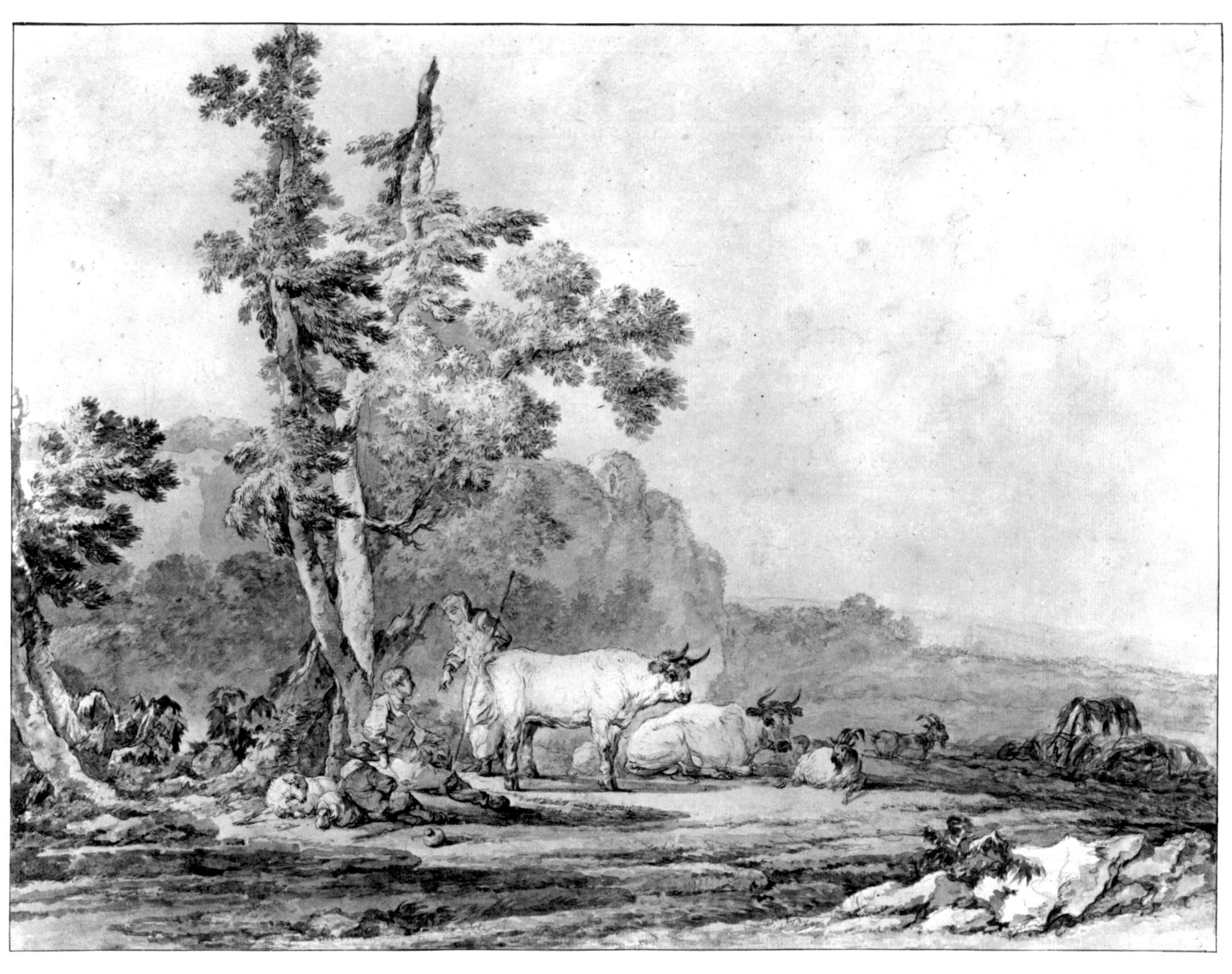

38a

ISAAC DE MOUCHERON

Amsterdam 1667–1744 Amsterdam

Imaginary Italianate Garden with Three Figures, Including One Transporting a Potted Shrub in a Boat

Pen and brown and gray ink, watercolor, over faint traces of black chalk. 9 1/8 x 13 3/8 inches (232 x 340 mm). Watermark: fragment of a coat of arms. Signed and dated at lower left, at base of urn, in point of brush and brown ink, *Moucheron Fecit / 1743*. Inscribed on old mount, in an eighteenth-century hand, in pen and brown ink, *I: Moucheron / 1743*; at lower edge of mount, in a later hand, in graphite, *Isaac Moucheron 1670–1744*.

PROVENANCE: David Carritt Limited, London; E. V. Thaw & Co., Inc., New York.

BIBLIOGRAPHY: PML/*FR* XX, 1984, pp. 280–81.

1982.91

After studying landscape painting with his father, Frederic, Isaac de Moucheron traveled to Italy in 1694, returning from Rome in 1697. While his skills as a landscape painter were considerable, he was also a printmaker. His work resembles that of his father but is perhaps more pleasing and, as is to be expected, more modern. The younger artist was often called upon to paint landscape staffage or backgrounds in the paintings of such artists as Gerard de Lairesse, Jakob de Wit, Adrian van der Velde, and Nicolaas Verkolje. His broad and facile manner also found him frequent employment as a decorator in the great houses of the wealthy Dutch patrons. One of his notable specialties was painting wall hangings for salons, which he decorated with parklike motifs and Arcadian landscapes. While most of his drawings are preparations for these wall hangings, he also executed many highly finished watercolors of the same genre, such as these two pavilion subjects, which seem to have been prepared with a view to a suite of engravings. These attractive watercolors can be found in many museums around the world, including the Rijksmuseum, the Louvre, the Albertina, Windsor Castle, and the Fitzwilliam Museum, Cambridge; fourteen are preserved in the Teyler Museum, Haarlem. The present drawings are perfect examples of the younger Moucheron's Italianate manner.

CDD

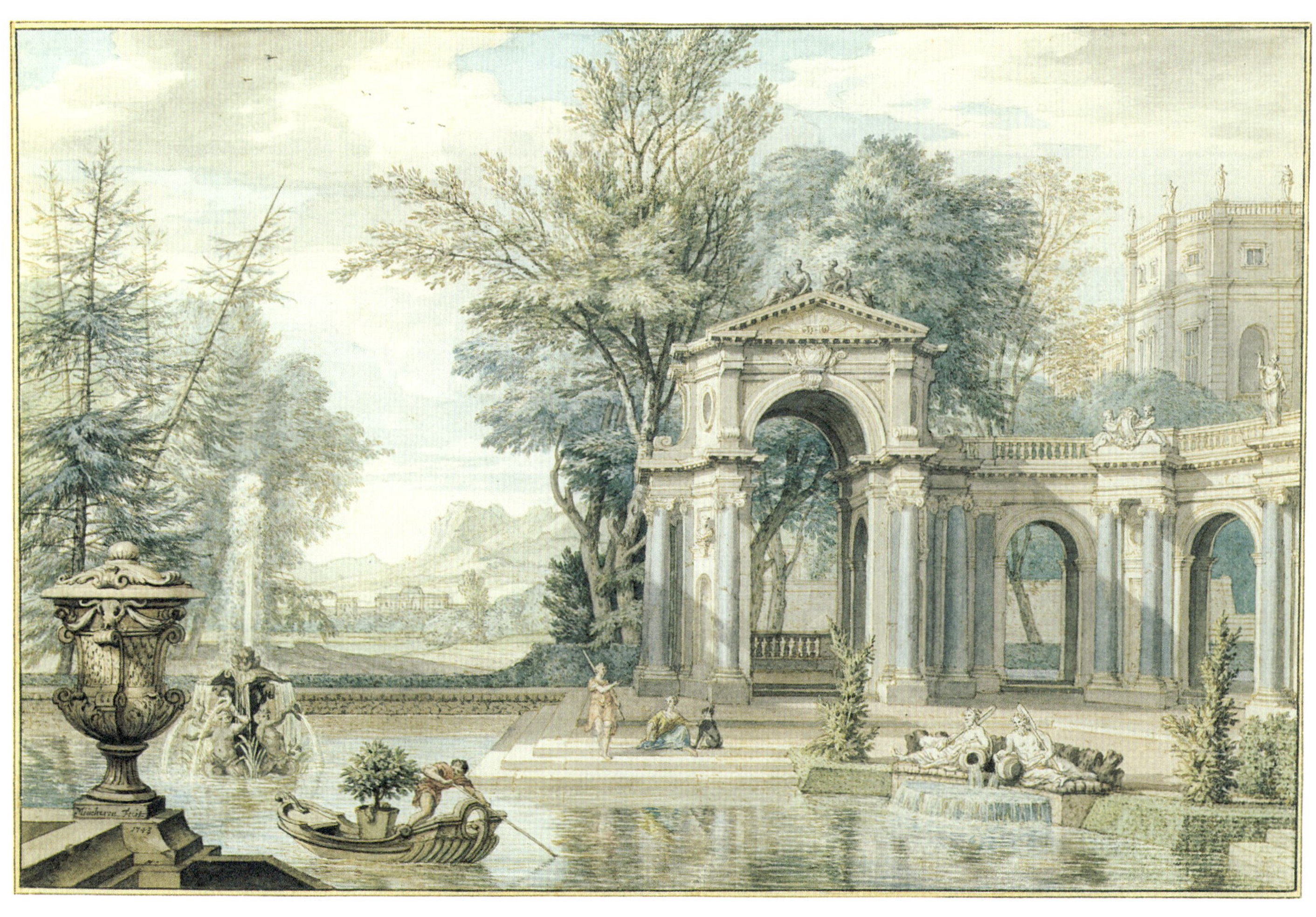

38b

Imaginary Italianate Garden with Four Figures and Two Dogs

Pen and brown and gray ink, watercolor, over faint traces of black chalk. 8 15/16 x 13 3/8 inches (226 x 339 mm). Watermark: none. Signed and dated at lower center, on pedestal at base of the stairway, in pen and brown ink, *Moucheron / Fecit 1743*.

PROVENANCE: A. Moriau (Lugt 1829 and 1853); Yvonne Tan Bunzl, London; E. V. Thaw & Co., Inc., New York.

BIBLIOGRAPHY: PML/*FR* XX, 1984, p. 281.

1982.92

See No. 38a.

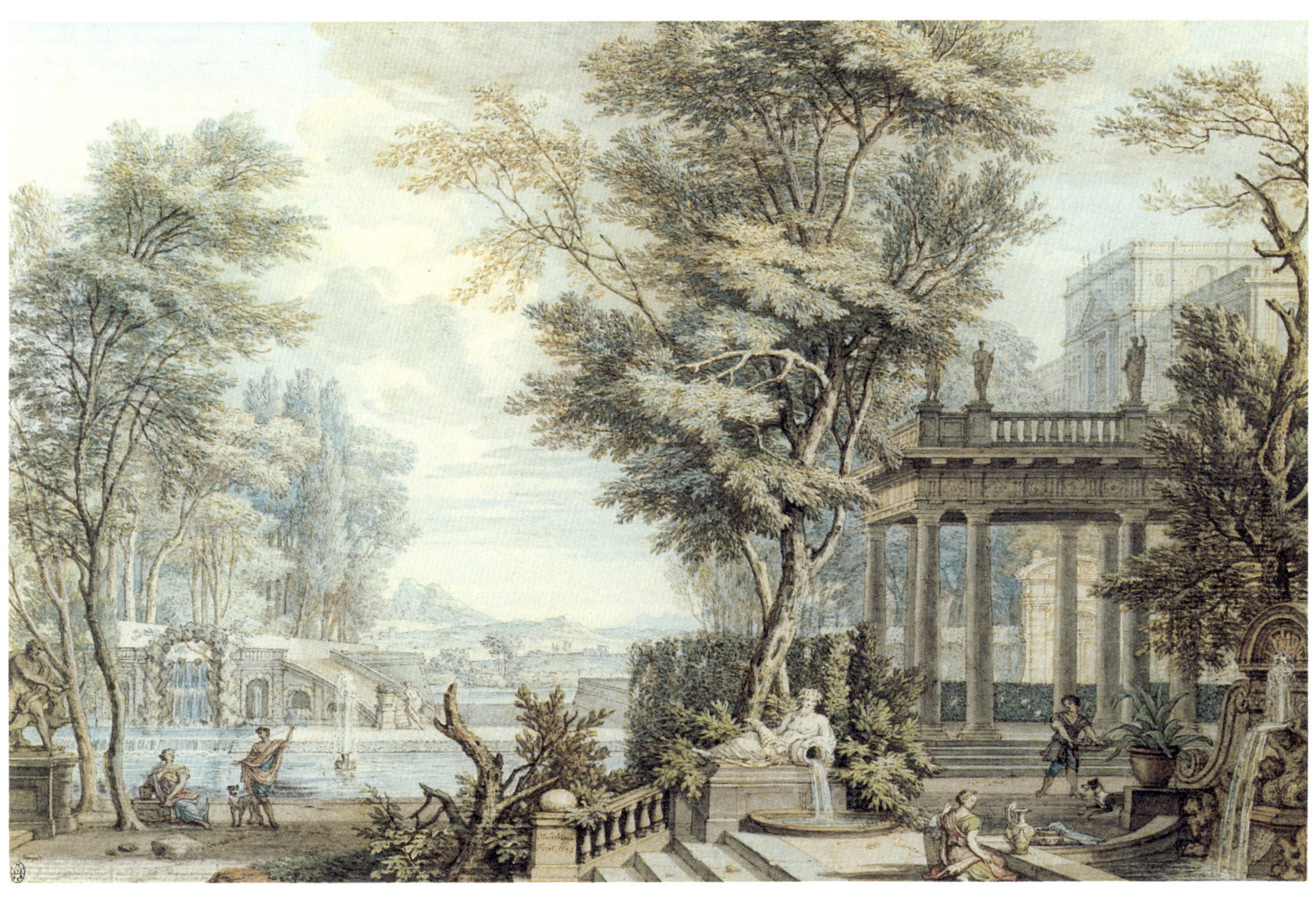

39

THOMAS JONES

Aberedw (Radnorshire, Wales) 1742–1803 Penkerrig, Radnorshire

View of the Villa of Maecenas and the Villa d'Este at Tivoli

Watercolor and some gouache over graphite. 11 1/4 x 16 15/16 inches (286 x 429 mm). Watermark: none. Signed, inscribed, and dated in sky, *Ruins of Mecenas's Villa & the Villa d'Este at Tivoli. T. Jones 1777*; variously inscribed with color notes.

PROVENANCE: possibly Mrs. Bethea Adams; her sale, London, Sotheby's, 26 July 1961, lot 61; Thos. Agnew & Sons Ltd., London.

EXHIBITIONS: London 1990, no. 9, repr.; New York PML 1992, no. 50, repr. (in color) p. 35; Montreal 1993, no. 72, repr.; Brussels 1994–95, no. 50, repr. (in color).

1990.15

Many of Jones's watercolors, with their careful observation of architecture and natural elements, come directly out of the English topographical tradition of landscape draughtsmanship. Using pencil, he first drew the architectural details across the middle of the sheet, finishing the composition with the classical framing device of a tree on the left. Both these formal qualities and to an extent the treatment of the foliage owe a great debt to Richard Wilson, with whom Jones studied from 1763 to 1765. Although Jones's use of watercolor departs from Wilson's standard black chalk technique, his almost monochromatic palette of blue-gray watercolor evokes the subdued tonalities of his master's chalk drawings. Jones's color notes inscribed on this sheet suggest that he may have intended to make a painting of the subject.

In November 1798, Jones completed his *Memoirs*, which were largely based on a diary he had kept for many years. According to the *Memoirs*, he arrived in Tivoli on 9 November 1777 and remained for about seven days, making sketches. His impressions of Tivoli and its landscape correspond closely to what is depicted in this view.

At Tivoli—the foaming Torrents rush down the Precipices into the deep Abyss with a fearful Noise and horrid Grandeur—The immense Masses of Stone rise abrupt—luxuriantly fringed with Shrubs and crowned with antique towers and Temples—Where the perpendicular & hanging Sides admit of no vegetation, & you discover the naked Rock—the Eye is charmed with the most beautiful variegated Tints—White, Grey, Red & Yellow—opposing, or blending their different Dyes together—But here is wanting the large Umbrageous Tree—to deck the foreground . . . ("Memoirs of Thomas Jones," intro. by A. Paul Oppé, Walpole Society *32 [1946–48], London, 1951, pp. 66–67).*

In the present drawing, the calculated addition of a foreground tree and the darker watercolor hues on the left are reminiscent not only of Wilson but also of Claude, whom Jones mentions later in the entry.

Other watercolors by Jones of the same subject, all of a similar size, are in the Fitzwilliam Museum, Cambridge; the Yale Center for British Art, New Haven; and the National Museum of Wales, Cardiff (see Whitworth Art Gallery, University of Manchester, *Travels in Italy, 1776–1783, Based on the Memoirs of Thomas Jones*, catalogue by Francis W. Hawcroft, 1988, nos. 50 and 51). Another watercolor view of the falls was recently sold at auction (sale, London, Sotheby's, 15 July 1993, lot 58, repr.). SW

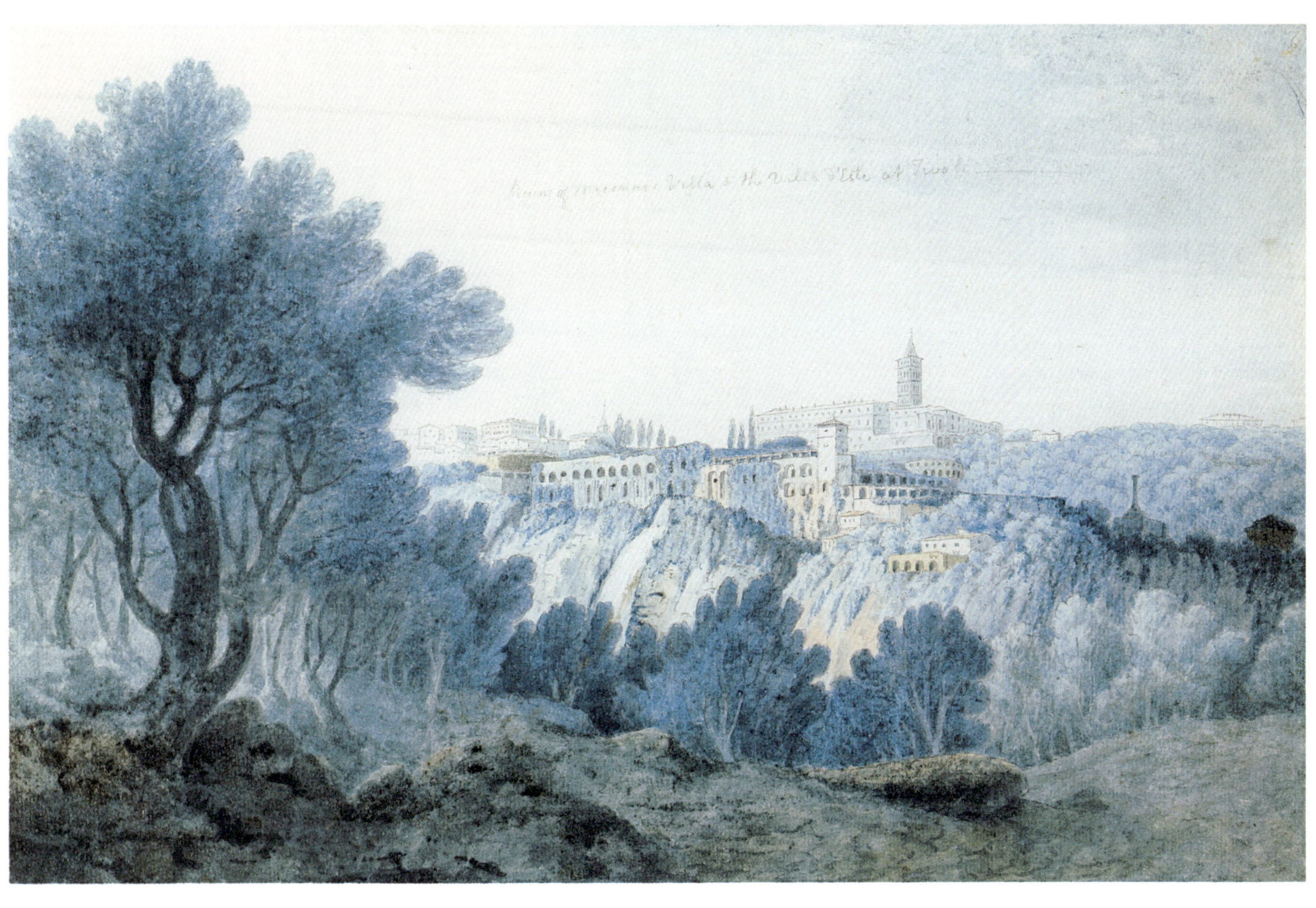

40

TIELEMAN CATO BRUINING

Nieuwkoop 1801–1877 The Hague

Three Drawings of the Interior of the Oranjezaal, Huis ten Bosch, The Hague

Watercolor, with ruled pen lines and gum arabic, over graphite. *The North Wall*: 17 3/16 x 17 3/16 inches (435 x 435 mm). *The East Wall*: 17 3/16 x 17 7/16 inches (436 x 442 mm). *The West Wall*: 17 3/16 x 17 7/16 inches (436 x 442 mm). Watermarks: none visible through lining.

PROVENANCE: Galerie Biedermann, Munich.

BIBLIOGRAPHY: New York and Richmond 1985–86, under no. 74; New York 1992, under no. 24.

1985.50:1–3

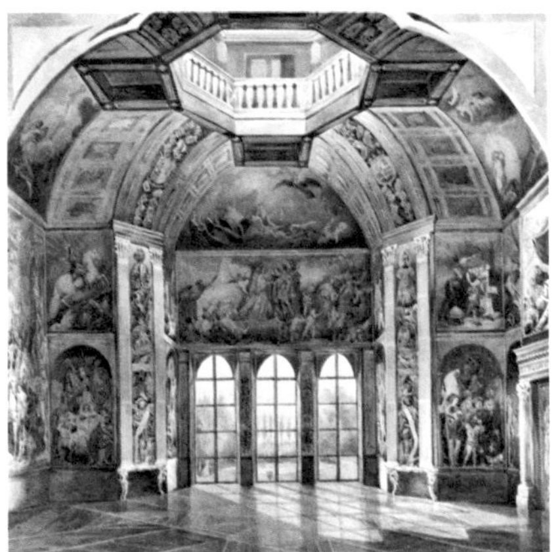

Fig. 1 Tieleman Cato Bruining, *Interior of the Oranjezaal, Huis ten Bosch*, Thaw Collection, The Pierpont Morgan Library.

These three drawings, treating the north, east, and west walls of the Oranjezaal, and a fourth, depicting the south, in the Thaw Collection (fig. 1), were purchased in 1985. At first the identity of the artist was unknown, but Dr. B. Woelderink and Mr. M. Loonstra of the Koninklijk Huisarchief connected these drawings with Bruining. In accordance with her usual custom of ordering watercolors of all the homes she occupied, Queen Sophie had commissioned a series of watercolor studies of the interior of the royal family's summer residence, Huis ten Bosch (literally "the house in the woods"), a moated seventeenth-century château just outside The Hague. The palace was built by Jann van Campen and Pieter Post between 1645 and 1652 for Amalia, wife of Prince Frederik Hendrik of Orange. Its main architectural feature is the octagonal Orange Hall, which stands forty-nine feet high. The documented series of Bruining's nine detail studies of the Oranjezaal commissioned by Queen Sophie are preserved in the Koninklijk Huisarchief, The Hague, and compare so closely to the series presently under discussion that they are undoubtedly by the same artist. Not much is known about Bruining, but he evidently made his living doing this sort of decorative architectural watercolor for which there was such a demand in the first half of the nineteenth century (see New York and Richmond 1985–86, under no. 74, for a discussion of this fashion).

The decoration of the Oranjezaal was devised by the humanist Constantin Huygens. While Huygens had not yet seen it, he almost certainly was inspired by Rubens's Marie de' Medici cycle in Paris and emulated it in his scheme for the Oranjezaal, in which the accomplishments of Prince Frederik Hendrik are celebrated. Like Rubens's Medici series, Huygens's scheme includes the story of Frederik Hendrik's government and marriage along with such subjects as the *Allegory on the Birth* (by Everdingen), with its references to the dawn of a new golden age, over the doorway on the east wall. Executed between 1648 and 1653, the decoration includes works by Honthorst, Everdingen, Jordaens, and Lievens. While there are paintings on three levels on almost every wall of the Oranjezaal, most of the west wall is taken up by Jordaens's *Triumph of Prince Frederik Hendrik*.

The iconography of the Oranjezaal was the subject of a published doctoral dissertation (H. Peter Raupp, *Die Ikonographie des Oranjezaal*, Hildesheim/New York, 1980), which was responded to at some length by B. Brenninkmeyer-De Rooij (in "Notities betreffende de decoratie van de Oranjezaal in Huis ten Bosch," *Oud Holland* 96, no. 3 [1982], pp. 133–90). CDD

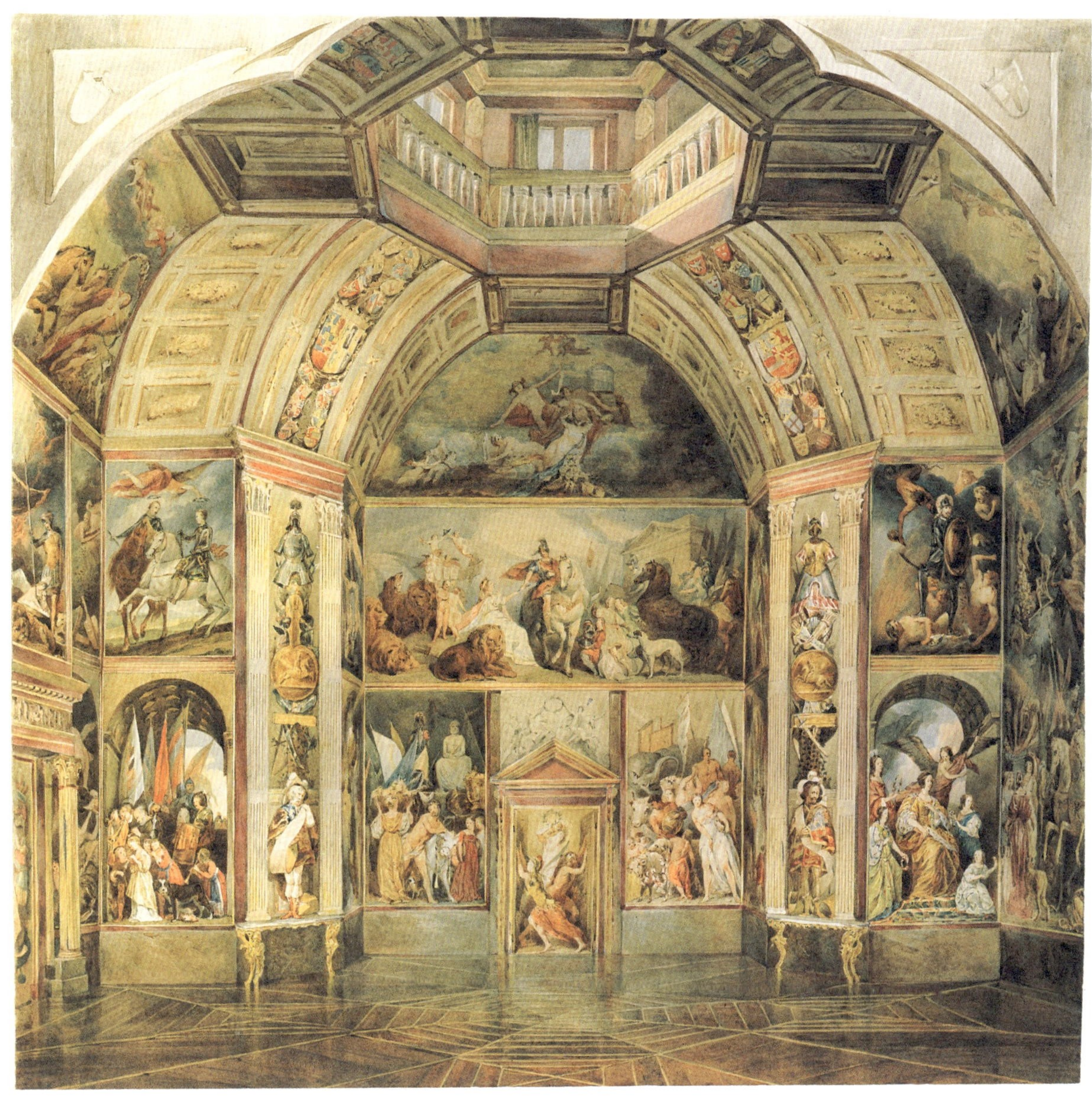

40a, North wall

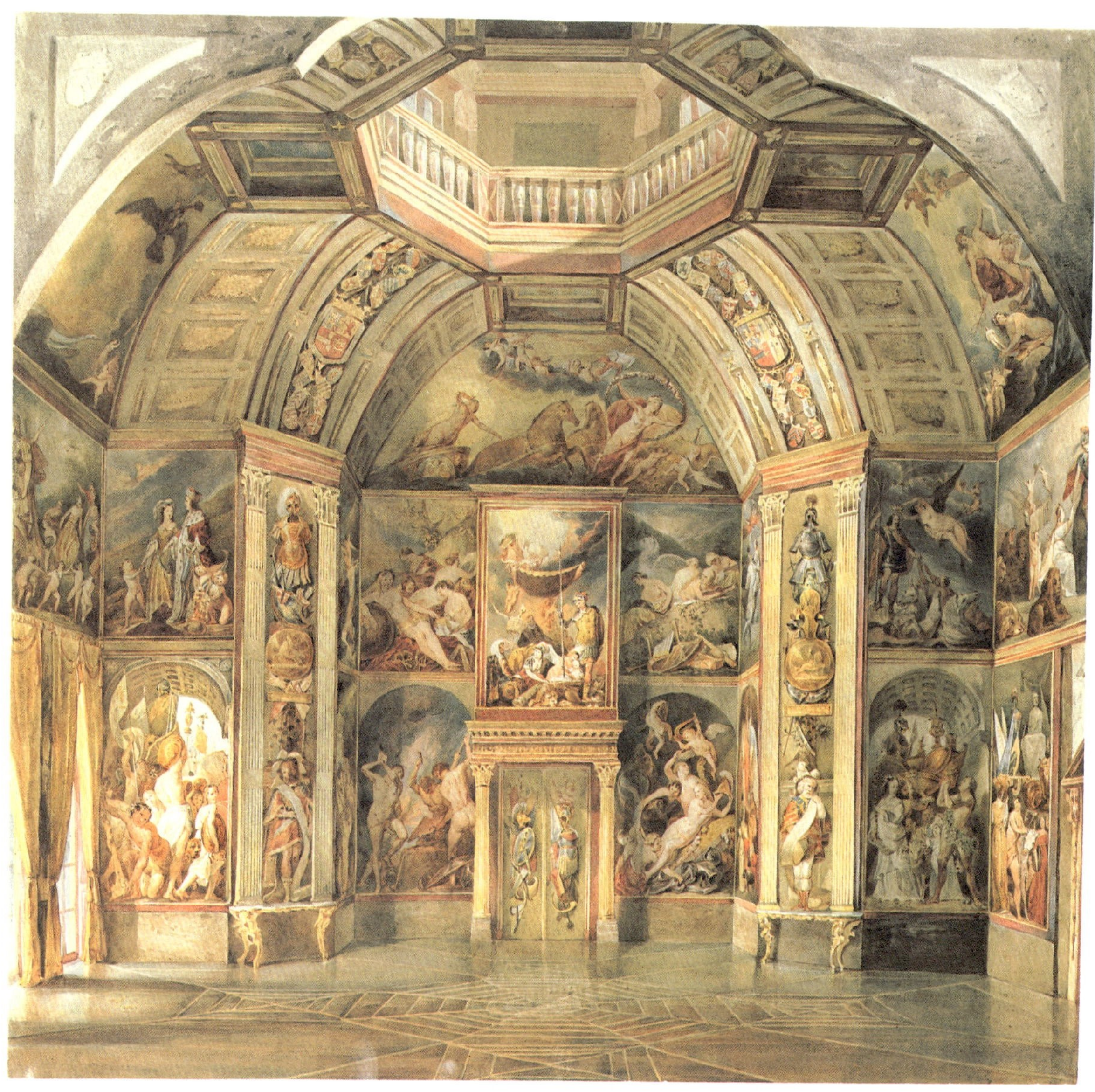

40b, East wall

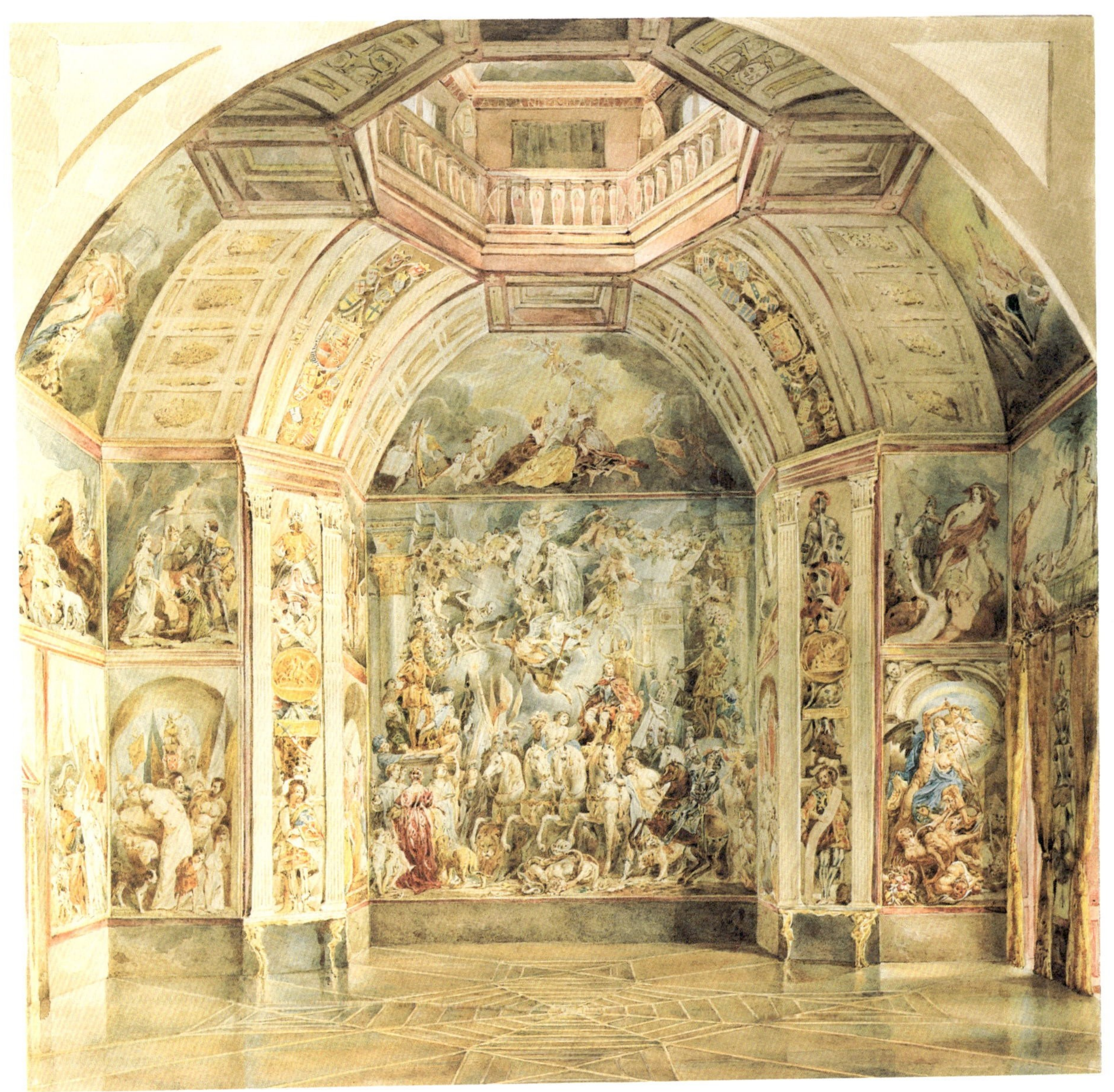

40c, West wall

Short Title References

Bibliography

AGNEW'S 1992
Agnew's, 1982–1992, London, 1992.

ANANOFF 1961
Alexandre Ananoff, *L'Œuvre dessiné de Jean-Honoré Fragonard (1732–1806)*, Paris, 1961.

ANANOFF 1966
Alexandre Ananoff, *L'Œuvre dessiné de François Boucher (1703–1770). Catalogue raisonné*, I, Paris, 1966.

ANANOFF AND WILDENSTEIN 1976
Alexandre Ananoff, with the collaboration of Daniel Wildenstein, *François Boucher*, 2 vols., Lausanne and Paris, 1976.

ART DIGEST 1950
"Detroit Sees France from David to Courbet," *Art Digest* 24, no. 1 (February 1950), p. 13.

ARTEMIS 1993
Artemis S. A., 1991–2, Luxembourg, 1993.

BEAN AND GRISWOLD 1990
Jacob Bean and William Griswold, *18th Century Italian Drawings in The Metropolitan Museum of Art*, New York, 1990.

BESNARD AND WILDENSTEIN 1928
Albert Besnard and Georges Wildenstein, *Latour*, Paris, 1928.

BRUAND AND HÉBERT 1970
Yves Bruand and Michèle Hébert, *Bibliothèque Nationale, Département des Estampes. Inventaires du fonds français: graveurs du XVIIIe siècle*, XI, Paris, 1970.

BYAM SHAW 1983
James Byam Shaw, *The Italian Drawings of the Frits Lugt Collection*, 3 vols., Paris, 1983.

CLARK 1963
Anthony M. Clark, "Pierleone Ghezzi's Portraits," *Paragone* 14, no. 165 (September 1963), pp. 11–21 (essay reprinted in *Studies in Roman Eighteenth-Century Painting*, Washington, D.C., 1981, pp. 11–19).

CONSTABLE AND LINKS 1976
W. G. Constable, *Canaletto: Giovanni Antonio Canal, 1697–1768*, 2d ed., rev. by J. G. Links, 2 vols., Oxford, 1976.

DACIER 1911
Emile Dacier, (notice) *Société de Reproduction des Dessins de Maîtres*, 3e année, Paris, 1911.

DACIER 1913
Emile Dacier, *Les Préparations de M.-Q. de La Tour, conservées dans les musées et les collections particulières*, Paris, 1913.

DACIER 1929–31
Edouard Emile Gabriel Dacier, *Gabriel de Saint-Aubin, peintre, dessinateur et graveur (1720–80)*, 2 vols., Paris and Brussels, 1929–31.

DACIER AND VUAFLART 1921–29
Emile Dacier and Albert Vuaflart, *Jean de Jullienne et les graveurs de Watteau au XVIIIe siècle*, 4 vols., Paris, 1921–29.

DESGUINE 1950
A. Desguine, *L'Œuvre de J.-B. Oudry sur le Parc et les Jardins d'Arcueil*, Paris, 1950.

DESHAIRS 1913
Léon Deshairs, "Les Arabesques de Watteau," *Archives de l'art français* 7 (1913).

DILKE 1902
Lady Dilke, *French Engravers and Draughtsmen of the 18th Century*, London, 1902.

EIDELBERG 1984
Martin Eidelberg, "Gabriel Huquier—Friend or Foe of Watteau?" *The Print Collector's Newsletter* 15, no. 5 (November–December 1984).

FLEURY AND BRIÈRE 1954
Elie Fleury and Gaston Brière, *Collection Maurice Quentin de La Tour à Saint-Quentin*, Saint-Quentin, 1954.

FOURCAUD 1908–9
L. de Fourcaud, "Antoine Watteau, peintre d'arabesques," *Revue de l'Art ancien et moderne* 13, no. 141 (December 1908), pp. 431–40; 14, no. 142 (January 1909), pp. 49–59; 15, no. 143 (February 1909), pp. 129–40.

FUHRING 1991
Peter Fuhring, "Valadier Drawings" (exhibition review), *Burlington Magazine* 133 (July 1991), p. 473.

GEORGE 1934
Waldemar George, "Portraits par Ingres et ses élèves," *La Renaissance de l'art français* 17 (October–November 1934), pp. 193–210.

GONCOURT 1875
Edmond de Goncourt, *Catalogue raisonné de l'œuvre peint, dessiné et gravé d'Antoine Watteau*, Paris, 1875.

GONCOURT 1881
Edmond de Goncourt, *La Maison d'un artiste*, I, Paris, 1881.

GRASSELLI 1993
Margaret Morgan Grasselli, "Eighteen Drawings by Antoine Watteau: A Chronological Study," *Master Drawings* 31, no. 2 (1993), pp. 103–27.

HENRIOT 1925
Gabriel Henriot, "La Collection David Weill," *L'Amour de l'art* 6 (January 1925), pp. 1–23.

HENRIOT 1927
Gabriel Henriot, *Collection David Weill, II: pastels, aquarelles, gouaches, tableaux modernes*, Paris, 1927.

JEAN-RICHARD 1978
Pierrette Jean-Richard, *L'Œuvre gravé de François Boucher dans la Collection Edmond de Rothschild*, Paris, 1978.

LAPAUZE 1911
Henry Lapauze, *Ingres: sa vie et son œuvre*, Paris, 1911.

MACGREGOR 1979
Neil MacGregor, "Roman Fashions, London" (exhibition review), *Burlington Magazine* 121 (November 1979), pp. 738–41.

MARIETTE 1851–60
P. J. Mariette, *Abecedario de P. J. Mariette et autres notes inédites de cet amateur sur les arts et les artistes*, compiled 1740–70; ed. Philippe de Chennevières and Anatole de Montaiglon, 6 vols., Paris, 1851–60.

MARIUZ 1982
Adriano Mariuz, *L'opera completa del Piazzetta*, Milan, 1982.

MASSENGALE 1993
Jean Montague Massengale, *Jean-Honoré Fragonard*, New York, 1993.

MICHEL 1889
A. Michel, *François Boucher suivi d'un catalogue raisonné de l'œuvre peint et dessiné* (1889), est. by Soullié with M. Ch. Masson, Paris, 1955.

MICHEL 1984
Marianne Roland Michel, *Watteau: An Artist of the Eighteenth Century*, Secaucus, New Jersey, 1984.

MICHEL 1987
Marianne Roland Michel, *Le Dessin français au XVIIIe siècle*, Fribourg, 1987.

NAEF 1970
Hans Naef, "Ingres frühe Profilbildnisse in Medaillenform," *Pantheon* 28, no. 3 (May–June 1970), pp. 221–36.

NAEF 1977–80
Hans Naef, *Die Bildniszeichnungen von J.-A.-D. Ingres*, 5 vols., Bern, 1977–80.

OPPERMAN 1977
Hal N. Opperman, *Jean-Baptiste Oudry*, 2 vols., New York, 1977.

PALLUCCHINI 1956
Rodolfo Pallucchini, *Piazzetta*, Milan, 1956.

PARKER AND MATHEY 1957
K. T. Parker and J. Mathey, *Antoine Watteau: catalogue complet de son œuvre dessiné*, 2 vols., Paris, 1957.

PML/FR
The Pierpont Morgan Library, *Report to the Fellows of The Pierpont Morgan Library*, New York, 1950–89. Reports edited by Frederick B. Adams, Jr., through 1968; by Charles Ryskamp, 1969 through 1986. Essays by Felice Stampfle, Cara D. Denison, and other members of the Department of Drawings and Prints.

PINTO 1980
John A. Pinto, "Nicola Michetti and Ephemeral Design in Eighteenth-Century Rome," in Henry A. Millon, ed., *Studies in Italian Art and Architecture, 15th through 18th Centuries, Memoirs of the American Academy in Rome*, XXXV, 1980, pp. 289–313.

PORTALIS AND BÉRALDI 1880–82
R. Portalis and H. Béraldi, *Les Graveurs du dix-huitième siècle*, 2 vols., Paris, 1880–82.

POSNER 1984
Daniel Posner, *Antoine Watteau*, Ithaca, New York, 1984.

RÉAU 1928
Louis Réau, *Les Dessins de Boucher*, Paris, 1928.

RICCI 1935
Seymour de Ricci, *Collection Albert Meyer*, Paris, 1935.

RICHARDSON 1979
John Richardson, ed., *The Collection of Germain Seligman: Paintings, Drawings, and Works of Art*, New York, Luxembourg, and London, 1979.

RUSSELL 1977
Francis Russell, "Salesroom Discoveries," *Burlington Magazine* 119 (February 1977), p. 153.

SÉRULLAZ 1969
Arlette Sérullaz, "Un album de croquis inédits de Jacques-Louis David," *Revue de l'art*, no. 5 (1969), pp. 65–68.

SÉRULLAZ 1981
Maurice Sérullaz, "Deux dessins de Watteau," *La Revue du Louvre*, no. 1 (1981), pp. 29–32.

SIEGFRIED 1990
Susan L. Siegfried, "The Artist as Nomadic Capitalist: The Case of Louis-Léopold Boilly," *Art History* 13, no. 4 (December 1990), pp. 516–41.

TOURNEUX 1904
Maurice Tourneux, "Collection de M. Jacques Doucet: pastels et dessins," *Les Arts* 36 (December 1904), pp. 1–5.

TOURNEUX 1908
Maurice Tourneux, "Exposition de cent pastels" (exhibition review), *Gazette des Beaux-Arts* 2 (1908), pp. 5–16.

VAILLAT AND RATOUIS 1923
Léandre Vaillat and Paul Ratouis de Limay, *J.-B. Perronneau: sa vie et son œuvre*, Paris and Brussels, 1923.

WILDENSTEIN 1923
Georges Wildenstein, *Un Peintre de paysage au XVIIIe siècle*, Paris, 1923.

Exhibitions

ANN ARBOR 1969
University of Michigan, Museum of Art, *The World of Voltaire*, 1969.

BALTIMORE 1941
Johns Hopkins University, *Landscape Painting from Patinir to Hubert Robert*, 1941.

BOSTON 1962
Museum of Fine Arts, *Fifty-one Watercolors and Drawings, John S. Newberry Collection*, 1962 (no catalogue).

BRUSSELS 1994–95
Musée Communal d'Ixelles, *Gainsborough to Ruskin: British Landscape Drawings & Watercolors from the Morgan Library*, catalogue by Cara D. Denison, Evelyn J. Phimister, and Stephanie Wiles, 1994–95.

CAMBRIDGE 1960
Fogg Art Museum, Harvard University, *Thirty-Three French Drawings from the Collection of John S. Newberry*, 1960.

CAMBRIDGE AND ELSEWHERE 1980
Fogg Art Museum, Harvard University, Malibu, J. Paul Getty Museum, and Montreal Museum of Fine Arts, *French Drawings from a Private Collection: Louis XIII to Louis XVI*, catalogue edited by Konrad Oberhuber and Beverly Schreiber Jacoby, 1980.

DETROIT 1950
Detroit Institute of Arts, *French Painting from David to Courbet*, 1950.

DETROIT 1951
Detroit Institute of Arts, *Recent Additions to the Collection of John S. Newberry*, 1951.

LONDON 1953
Royal Academy of Arts, *Drawings by the Old Masters*, 1953.

LONDON 1962
Arts Council Gallery, *Old Master Drawings from the Collection of Mr. C. R. Rudolf*, 1962.

LONDON 1978
David Carritt Limited, *18th Century French Paintings, Drawings and Sculpture*, 1978.

LONDON 1980
British Museum, *Watteau: Drawings in the British Museum*, catalogue by Paul Hulton, 1980.

LONDON 1982
Sotheby's *Preview*, London, 1982.

LONDON 1989
Thos. Agnew & Sons, Ltd., *Master Drawings & Sculpture*, 1989.

LONDON 1990
Thos. Agnew & Sons, Ltd., *English Watercolours and Drawings*, 1990.

LONDON 1990A
Duke Street Gallery, Yvonne Tan Bunzl and Kate de Rothschild, *Master Drawings*, 1990.

LONDON 1990B
Harari & Johns, Katrin Bellinger, *Meisterzeichnungen / Master Drawings 1500–1900*, 1990.

LONDON 1990C
Trinity Fine Art, *Architectural and Decorative Drawings*, 1990.

LONDON 1991
Artemis Group (David Carritt Limited), *Valadier, Three Generations of Roman Goldsmiths: An Exhibition of Drawings and Works of Art*, 1991.

MIDDLETOWN AND BALTIMORE 1975
Davison Art Center, Wesleyan University, and Baltimore Museum of Art, *Prints and Drawings by Gabriel de Saint-Aubin: 1724–1780*, catalogue by Victor Carlson, Ellen D'Oench, and Richard S. Field, 1975.

MINNEAPOLIS 1961
University Gallery, University of Minnesota, *The Eighteenth Century: One Hundred Drawings by One Hundred Artists*, catalogue by Hylton Thomas, 1961.

MONTREAL 1993
Centre Canadien d'Architecture, *Exploring Rome: Piranesi and His Contemporaries*, catalogue by Cara D. Denison, Myra Nan Rosenfeld, and Stephanie Wiles, 1993.

NEW YORK 1938
Wildenstein and Co., *French Eighteenth-Century Pastels, Water-Colors and Drawings from the David-Weill Collection*, 1938.

NEW YORK 1961
Galerie Paul Rosenberg, *Ingres in American Collections*, 1961.

NEW YORK 1962
Stephen Spector, *Old Master Drawings*, 1962.

NEW YORK 1964
Charles E. Slatkin Galleries, *Fair Ladies*, 1964.

NEW YORK 1971
The Metropolitan Museum of Art, *Drawings from New York Collections, III: The Eighteenth Century in Italy*, catalogue by Jacob Bean and Felice Stampfle, 1971.

NEW YORK 1984
Didier Aaron, *French Master Drawings*, catalogue by Alan E. Salz, 1984.

NEW YORK 1990
P. & D. Colnaghi, Ltd., *Claude to Corot: The Development of Landscape Painting in France*, catalogue edited by Alan Wintermute, 1990.

NEW YORK 1992
The Frick Collection, *An Album of Nineteenth-Century Interiors: Watercolors from Two Private Collections*, catalogue by Charlotte Gere, New York, 1992.

NEW YORK AND ELSEWHERE 1986–87
The Metropolitan Museum of Art, Detroit Institute of Arts, and Paris, Grand Palais, *François Boucher 1703–1770*, 1986–87.

NEW YORK AND ELSEWHERE 1993
New York, Paris, and London, Kate de Rothschild and Didier Aaron, *Master Drawings*, 1993.

NEW YORK AND RICHMOND 1985–86
New York, The Pierpont Morgan Library, and Richmond, Virginia Museum of Fine Arts, *Drawings from the Collection of Mr. & Mrs. Eugene Victor Thaw*, Part II, catalogue by Cara D. Denison, William W. Robinson, Julia Herd, and Stephanie Wiles, 1985–86.

NEW YORK PML 1981
The Pierpont Morgan Library, *European Drawings, 1375–1825*, catalogue by Cara D. Denison and Helen B. Mules, with the assistance of Jane V. Shoaf, 1981.

NEW YORK PML 1984
The Pierpont Morgan Library, *French Drawings, 1550–1825*, catalogue by Cara D. Denison, 1984.

NEW YORK PML 1989
The Pierpont Morgan Library, *Exploring Rome: Piranesi and His Contemporaries*, 1989 (no catalogue).

NEW YORK PML 1992
The Pierpont Morgan Library, *Sketching at Home and Abroad: British Landscape Drawings, 1750–1850*, 1992.

NICE AND ELSEWHERE 1977
Musée Chéret, Clermont-Ferrand, Musée Bargoin, Nancy, Musée des Beaux-Arts, *Carle van Loo, 1705–1765*, catalogue by Marie C. Sahut, 1977.

OMAHA 1941
Joslyn Art Museum, *Tenth Anniversary Exhibition*, 1941 (no catalogue).

PARIS 1908
Galerie Georges Petit, *Cent Pastels*, 1908.

PARIS 1924
Galerie Balzac, *De David à Manet*, 1924.

PARIS 1925
Hôtel Charpentier, *Exposition de Saint-Aubin*, 1925.

PARIS 1927
Hôtel Charpentier, *Exposition de pastels français du XVIIe et du XVIIIe siècle*, catalogue by Emile Dacier, 1927.

PARIS 1929
Galerie Georges Petit, *Comte Pierre de Jumilhac et divers*, 1929.

PARIS 1933
Galerie André Weil, *Exposition Carmontelle*, 1933.

PARIS 1933A
Wildenstein and Co., *De Goncourt Exhibition*, 1933.

PARIS 1934
Galerie Jacques Seligmann, *Portraits par Ingres et ses élèves*, 1934.

PARIS 1935
Jean A. Seligman, *Dessins du dix-huitième siècle, Collection Albert Meyer*, 1935.

PARIS 1984
Musée du Louvre, *Dessins et sciences: XVIIe*, 1984.

PARIS 1987
Musée du Louvre, *Dessins français du XVIIIe siècle de Watteau à Lemoyne*, catalogue by Roseline Bacou, Lise Duclaux, Hélène Guicharnaud, and Jean-François Méjanès, 1987.

PARIS AND AMSTERDAM 1964
Institut Néerlandais and Amsterdam, Rijksmuseum, Prentenkabinet, *Le Dessin français de Claude à Cézanne dans les collections hollandaises*, 1964.

PARIS AND ELSEWHERE 1991–92
Grand Palais, Philadelphia Museum of Art, and Fort Worth, Kimbell Art Museum, *The Loves of the Gods: Mythological Painting from Watteau to David*, catalogue by Colin B. Bailey, with the assistance of Carrie A. Hamilton, 1991–92.

PARIS AND NEW YORK 1991
Haboldt & Co., *Dessins anciens des écoles du nord, françaises et italiennes*, 1991.

PARIS AND NEW YORK 1993–94
Musée du Louvre and New York, The Pierpont Morgan Library, *French Master Drawings from The Pierpont Morgan Library*, catalogue by Cara Dufour Denison, 1993–94.

PARIS AND VERSAILLES 1989–90
Musée du Louvre and Versailles, Musée National du Château, *Jacques Louis David, 1748–1825*, catalogue by Antoine Schnapper and Arlette Sérullaz, 1989–90.

PITTSBURGH 1951
Carnegie Institute, *French Painting, 1100–1900*, 1951.

PROVIDENCE 1931
Museum of Art, Rhode Island School of Design, *French Painting*, 1931.

ROME 1991
Palazzo Ruspoli, *Il Segno del Genio: Centro disegni di grandi Maestri del passato dall'Ashmolean Museum di Oxford*, catalogue by Christopher White, Catherine Whistler, and Colin Harrison, 1991.

SAINTE-FOY-LA-GRANDE 1970
Château Richelieu, *Expo d'art*, 1970.

STORRS 1973
William Benton Museum (Conn.), *The Academy of Europe: Rome in the 18th Century*, catalogue by Frederick den Broeder, 1973.

TORONTO AND ELSEWHERE 1972–73
Art Gallery of Ontario, Ottawa, National Gallery of Canada, San Francisco, California Palace of the Legion of Honor, and New York Cultural Center, *French Master Drawings of the 17th and 18th Centuries in North American Collections*, catalogue by Pierre Rosenberg, 1972–73.

VENICE 1983
Fondazione Giorgio Cini, *G. B. Piazzetta: disegni, incisioni, libri manoscritti*, catalogue by George Knox et al., 1983.

WASHINGTON 1983–84
National Gallery of Art, *Piazzetta: A Tercentenary Exhibition of Drawings, Prints, and Books*, catalogue by George Knox, 1983–84.

WASHINGTON 1988–89
National Gallery of Art and The Phillips Collection, *The Pastoral Landscape: The Legacy of Venice and the Modern Vision*, catalogue by Robert C. Cafritz, Lawrence Gowing, and David Rosand, 1988–89.

WASHINGTON AND CHICAGO 1973–74
National Gallery of Art and Art Institute of Chicago, *François Boucher in North American Collections: 100 Drawings*, catalogue by Regina Shoolman Slatkin, 1973–74.

WASHINGTON AND ELSEWHERE 1984–85
National Gallery of Art, Paris, Grand Palais, and Berlin, Schloss Charlottenburg, *Watteau, 1684–1721*, catalogue by Margaret Morgan Grasselli and Pierre Rosenberg, 1984–85.

Index of Artists

PUBLISHED BY
THE PIERPONT MORGAN LIBRARY
Julianne Griffin, *Publisher*
Patricia Emerson, *Editorial Coordinator*
Noah Chasin, *Publications Administrator*
Deborah Winard, *Publications Associate*

PROJECT STAFF
Cara Dufour Denison, *Curator, Department of Drawings and Prints*
Stephanie Wiles, *Associate Curator, Department of Drawings and Prints*
Ruth S. Kraemer, *Research Assistant, Department of Drawings and Prints*
David A. Loggie, *Chief Photographer*
Edward J. Sowinski, *Assistant, Photography Department*
Marilyn Palmeri, *Administrator, Photographic Services, Rights and Reproductions*
David Coleman, *Associate, Photographic Services, Rights and Reproductions*
Patricia Reyes, *Mellon Conservator*
Mary Cropley, *Assistant Conservator*
Timothy Herstein, *Assistant, Conservation Department*

DESIGN AND TYPOGRAPHY
Catherine Waters, New Haven, Connecticut

TYPESETTING
Highwood Typographic Services, Hamden, Connecticut

PRINTING
Hull Printing Company, Meriden, Connecticut

BINDING
Mueller Trade Bindery, Meriden, Connecticut